99

Great Answers to Everyone's Investment Questions

By
**Linda Bryant, Diane Pearl
and Ellie Williams**

The *MONEYWISE* Partners

CAREER PRESS
180 Fifth Avenue
P.O. Box 34
Hawthorne, NJ 07507
1-800-CAREER-1
201-427-0229 (outside U.S.)
FAX: 201-427-2037

99 GREAT ANSWERS TO EVERYONE'S INVESTMENT QUESTIONS
ISBN 1-56414-061-X, $10.95
Cover design by A Good Thing, Inc.
Photography by Joe Berman
Printed by Bookmart Press

To order this title by mail, please include price as noted above, $2.50 handling per order, and $1.00 for each book ordered. Send to: Career Press, Inc., 180 Fifth Ave., P.O. Box 34, Hawthorne, NJ 07507

Or call toll-free 1-800-CAREER-1 (Canada: 201-427-0229) to order using VISA or MasterCard, or for further information on books from Career Press.

Library of Congress Cataloging-in-Publication Data

Bryant, Linda, 1946-
  99 great answers to everyone's investment questions / by Linda Bryant, Diane Pearl, and Ellie Williams.
      p.   cm.
  Includes index.
  ISBN 1-56414-061-X : $10.95
  1. Investments.   2. Finance, Personal.   I. Pearl, Diane, 1957-
II. Williams, Ellie, 1962-   . III. Title.   IV. Title: Ninety
  nine great answers to everyone's investment questions.
HG4521.B765   1993
332.6--dc20   93-21726
                                                                CIP

Acknowledgments

To all our **MONEYWISE** workshop graduates, who believe that the key to getting great answers is knowing the right questions to ask. And to our families for their love and support.

Ellie, Di and Linda

Contents

No One Will Watch Your Money Like You Will

It's been said, "You don't have to know all the right answers if you know all the right questions." Now you have the questions to ask right at your fingertips.

The questions seldom change, but the answers change with tomorrow's market. This is why we wrote this book. Use it every time you do something with money; and you will save yourself time, money and heartache.

Moneywise Tip

If you can't spend the time, don't spend your money.

The questions in this book will help you arrive at better decisions, and make more effective use of financial advice and advisors. You will be able to tell your advisor what you want, just like you would if you were selecting a new car.

You wouldn't make a buying decision without knowing the size, color, features and the cost of a major purchase. This book will make it easier for you to gather critical financial information and to be knowledgeable and self-confident about your financial decisions.

This book will *not* make you a financial expert; no book can do that. We use the questions to show you the "inside story" of investments and insurance: how they work and how they are sold. By becoming familiar and comfortable with these questions, you will be able to get better, more complete information about your money. You will learn what it really costs to invest—including the fees that are disclosed, and the fees you never hear about. Then you will know whether what you buy is good for *you* or good for the person who is selling it.

MONEYWISE is a financial training and education company based in St. Louis, Mo. As its three partners, we teach skills that last a lifetime and explain how making money and *keeping* money are two different concepts requiring separate sets of skills. Just because you are good at making money, doesn't make you good at keeping it. Through our varied experiences in the banking and brokerage worlds, we tell the "inside story" and take the mystery out of money.

This book is based on our methodology of teaching people what they really want to know; the right questions to ask about money. Using the questions, people can get the answers and evaluate the answers for themselves.

Ellie Williams graduated *magna cum laude* in finance from the University of Missouri-Columbia. She has eight years of banking and brokerage experience, ranging from securities trading and investment advisory to managing a St. Louis brokerage firm. Ellie developed *Investing 1-2-3,* a **MONEYWISE** workshop, which teaches a framework for investing and evaluating advice from brokers and planners by knowing the right questions to ask. She is an experienced investment advisor and holds six securities licenses.

Linda Bryant earned a bachelor of science business administration in finance from The Ohio State University and has more than 20 years of experience in finance in a variety of industries. She has worked extensively with individual investors and has been an innovator in the concept of impartial financial education. She developed the *MONEY-WISE Building for Retirement* Workshop. Linda has addressed audiences including national conferences and universities. She holds six securities licenses.

Diane Pearl graduated from Lake Land College with an associate degree in retail management. As investment club director for a major bank, her main concern was ongoing investment education for club membership. She developed the concept for *Organize with MONEYWISE*, a 90-page guide designed to simplify record-keeping, consolidate important documents and create a complete personal financial handbook. At age 20, Diane established and operated a retail business. She acquired her interest in financial education during her three years as a securities broker. She holds four securities licenses.

We hope you will read the entire book before you delve into and use any one chapter. It is important for you to read the overview of all investment alternatives in Chapters 1 through 4 before you focus on the investments that best meet your needs. Therefore, this book provides the first 99 questions to ask—of yourself and of any prospective financial advisor.

Ask the questions—and get the answers, because no one will watch your money like you will!

—The *MONEYWISE* Partners

Chapter 1

Step 1: Identify Where You Are

It's 6:30 p.m. and you are sitting down to a quiet dinner with your family when the phone rings. It's a broker from one of the big investment firms. You've never met him before, but he's calling you with a "great buy" on a new stock issue. You have to make the decision tonight; he says they'll be sold out tomorrow. Should you buy a few shares? How do you know if this is a good investment for you?

Follow the three steps to successful financial decision-making. The first is to identify where you are; second, where you are going; and third, how to get there. The *where you are* step requires you to compile a list of your investible funds and know exactly what you own. *Where you are going* is deciding what your goals are. *How to get there* is the actual buying and selling of Certificates of Deposit (CDs), insurance, stocks, bonds, mutual funds, etc., in order to reach those goals. Most of the questions in this book deal with Step 3: how to get there.

As in any step-by-step process, you can't take Step 2 until Step 1 is completed. In other words, you need to learn where you are, before you can decide where to go. Choosing investment products is how to get there. Without knowing where you *are* or where you are *going*, how can you think about buying an investment that will get you there? Take it one step at a time. The three-step investment process will become easier once you understand two things: total return and the investment pyramid.

Total return is the bottom line

One of the first things many people ask about an investment is, "How much will I make?" Or, "What is the return?" There are many types of return: current yield, yield to maturity, capital gains, interest, dividends, etc. Unfortunately, they are all different and are all related to different types of investments. Sound confusing?

There are several expressions that refer to the growth of the original investment you make: growth of principal, capital appreciation, increase in investment, price appreciation, etc. Each refers to the growth in the original money you invested. Several other terms such as current yield, interest rate and dividend rate refer to income received during the life of an investment. How then, can you compare unlike investments such as stocks, bonds, mutual funds, and CDs? Use *total return*.

Total return will be one of your most valuable tools in making investment decisions. What you really need to know to make the best decision is how the investment's price has changed and what income it has generated over the last year, 5 years and 10 years. The sum of these two items is total return. It tells you how the investment has performed over time, not just how it is performing now. That is what is important. Even though past data is no guarantee of future performance, it is valuable material.

	Gain or loss of principal in original investment
plus	Interest or dividends received
equals	**Total return**

Think of the total return of an investment as you would the life of a maple tree. The tree yields lumber at maturity and sap throughout its lifetime. The tree can be struck by lighting, resulting in a total loss, or it can grow to maturity (as can the principal of an investment); the sap from the tree (income) comes at intervals throughout its lifetime. The total return from the tree is the sum of its yield in lumber and its yield of sap.

Here is an example of how total return works, using three different investments: a CD, ABC Company common stock, and Joe's Biotech Company bonds.[1] The assumptions, *only for the purpose of this example*, are:

1. We invest $1,000 in each and agree to redeem or sell them one year from today.
2. All three investments pay interest or dividends as promised.
3. ABC Company common stock price increases 10 percent during the next year.
4. Joe's Biotech Company has a bad year; at the end of the year the bond is worth only $500.

With the example on page 12, you can see why you should *never* base a decision solely on the current return figures of 5.5 percent, 2 percent or 18 percent given to you in the beginning.

---

[1] A corporate bond is a promissory note to repay the face value to the owner at a specific future date.

11

	CD FDIC Insured	ABC Stock	Joe's Biotech Bond
Original investment Assumption #1	$1,000	$1,000	$1,000
Interest: Dividend:	5.5%	2%	18%
One year later: Return of original investment	$1,000	Assum. #3 $1,100	Assum. #4 $500
Income Assumption #2	$55	$20	$180
Total dollars returned	$1,055	$1,120	$680
TOTAL RETURN	+5.5%	+12%	-32%

Moneywise Tip

Always use total return to compare investment alternatives.

Should you make investment decisions based solely on promised total return? No. You should also consider the risk/reward relationship of the investment and how it affects your *Personal Pyramid*, which you'll read about next. To prepare for that step, let's examine the traditional investment pyramid, which simplifies all investments by dividing them into five categories.

1. What is the investment pyramid?

It would be very frustrating to try to put the pieces of a puzzle together without first seeing a copy of the finished picture. It would not be fun; it would take too long; and you would make a lot of mistakes. It's the same with your Personal Pyramid. The investment pyramid in this chapter, and the story about Jane's Personal Pyramid in the next chapter will help you form the picture you need. In just a few minutes (not hours, not days) you will be able to begin working examples with your own money.

The investment pyramid represents all levels of risk and reward. We recommend a five-level investment pyramid, because it has enough levels (categories of risk) to give you (on a scale of one to five) an idea of the amount of risk you are taking.

Moneywise Tip

Turn to the investment pyramid before you invest; before you enter any investment discussion. Use it as a reference and you'll know if an investment fits your needs.

How is this done? Every investment can be assigned to one of these five levels of risk. If you write down every investment you own and learn how to determine in which level each belongs, you can assess whether you are taking the most conservative risk (Level 1), a conservative risk (Level 2), a moderate risk (Level 3), an aggressive risk (Level 4), or a speculative risk (Level 5). *Never assume you are not taking any risk at all.* Even with cash, there is the risk that you might lose it, or that it will not buy as much as it would have when you first hid it under the mattress!

The risk you are taking increases with each higher level of the pyramid. The higher the total return promised on an investment, the higher its level of the pyramid. The pyramid is important because it is difficult to keep current with today's complex market. This model helps you evaluate risk and make decisions that could save you time and money.

- *How can I determine in which level of the pyramid a particular investment belongs?*
- *How much of my investible funds should I have invested in each level of the pyramid?*

In the investment pyramid we are addressing your "investible funds"—all your assets *except* your primary residence and any art, jewelry or collectibles, unless they are "for sale." Investible funds include stocks, bonds, mutual funds, cash value of life insurance policies, the money you put aside for emergencies and retirement—everything you own to generate income or growth. Each of your investments can be categorized in one level of the pyramid. The result is *your* Personal Pyramid.

Moneywise Tip

Remember, the greater the promised total return, the greater the investment risk and the more you need to know about the investment before you buy or sell.

The Investment Pyramid

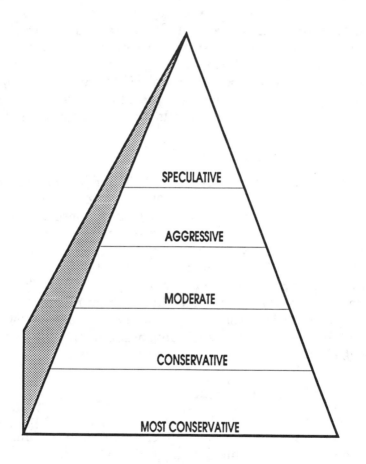

Level 1: Most conservative risk

This is your foundation, where you will keep your emergency cash reserves. The investment objective with these funds is to provide income and insure preservation of principal. These investments are short-term, have high liquidity and low total return. Examples are cash, money market accounts, CDs, U.S. government securities, and commercial paper. Your total return will be interest, not price appreciation. Keep *15 percent* or less of your investible funds invested in this level during any financial stage of life. Your emergency reserves should equal six months of living expenses. If that would require more than 15 percent of your investible funds, then you should exceed the 15 percent.

Level 2: Conservative risk

These investments are often held for longer periods of time; they carry a little more risk, promise a little more reward, and may have less liquidity than those in Level 1. Your objective with these investments is to provide income. Examples are U.S. Government zero coupon bonds, insured municipal bonds, unit investment trusts, fixed annuities and some U.S. Government bond mutual funds. Total return will be mostly interest plus or minus some price change. Keep between *15 percent and 45 percent* of your investible funds in this level, depending upon your financial stage of life.

Level 3: Moderate risk

These investments are for moderate growth and income. You may need to hold these investments *longer* than those in Levels 1 and 2 to make your projected total return. Total return is expected to come from moderate change in principal and modest income. Investments are growth-oriented, thus, their prices will fluctuate and they may be less liquid.

The Investment Pyramid-
Example Investments

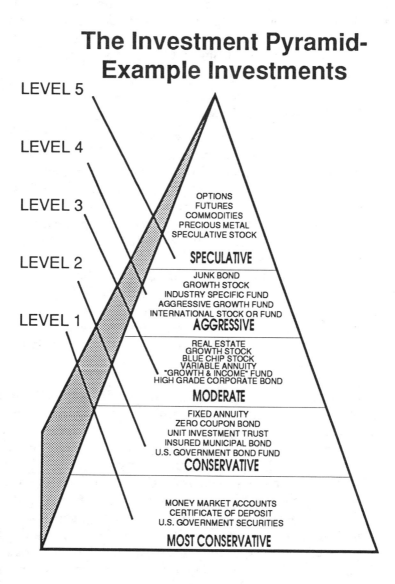

LEVEL 5

LEVEL 4

LEVEL 3

LEVEL 2

LEVEL 1

OPTIONS
FUTURES
COMMODITIES
PRECIOUS METAL
SPECULATIVE STOCK

SPECULATIVE

JUNK BOND
GROWTH STOCK
INDUSTRY SPECIFIC FUND
AGGRESSIVE GROWTH FUND
INTERNATIONAL STOCK OR FUND

AGGRESSIVE

REAL ESTATE
GROWTH STOCK
BLUE CHIP STOCK
VARIABLE ANNUITY
"GROWTH & INCOME" FUND
HIGH GRADE CORPORATE BOND

MODERATE

FIXED ANNUITY
ZERO COUPON BOND
UNIT INVESTMENT TRUST
INSURED MUNICIPAL BOND
U.S. GOVERNMENT BOND FUND

CONSERVATIVE

MONEY MARKET ACCOUNTS
CERTIFICATE OF DEPOSIT
U.S. GOVERNMENT SECURITIES

MOST CONSERVATIVE

Examples of investments in this level are high-grade corporate bonds, variable annuities, mutual funds in the "growth and income" category, some stocks (such as blue chip stocks) and real estate. Keep between *25 percent and 35 percent* of your investible funds in the moderate level during any financial stage of life.

Level 4: Aggressive risk

These investments are for growth in principal. Total return comes primarily from changes in principal value. There is little or no dividend income from common stocks in this level. High-coupon rate bonds and some limited partnerships may provide high income to accompany the high risk of price change. Investments in this level carry significant risk along with equally significant projected total return. (You can't have one without the other.) They may be very volatile or have very low liquidity, both of which can mean risk to your principal if you have to sell quickly.

Examples of aggressive investments are low-grade corporate bonds, some growth stocks, industry-specific mutual funds (oil, health care, high-tech), mutual funds labeled "aggressive growth," international stocks, international bonds and international mutual funds.

Did you notice that growth stocks are in both the moderate and aggressive levels of the pyramid? This is because an investment can change levels of the pyramid, depending upon its performance; so it is important to review frequently how and where your money is invested.

Money-center bank stocks are an example of stocks that changed from moderate to aggressive in the late 1980s. With general unrest in the banking industry, these stocks took on the characteristics of aggressive-level stocks (high stock price volatility, sporadic earnings or lack of earnings).

Keep between *15 percent and 40 percent* of your investible funds in this level during any financial stage of life.

Level 5: Speculative risk

Only when you have money you can afford to lose, can you invest in the speculative level. If you win, it's a thrill; if you lose, it won't change your life. Unfortunately, this is where careless investors are most often abused. These investments are risky; and though they make great cocktail party conversations, most people pay dearly for them. You hear about the gains, but do you ever hear about the losses?

Total return in this level comes from price change (which can go to zero as quickly as it can reach the sky), rarely from income. Examples are futures, options, commodities, precious metals, speculative stocks and penny stocks (stocks priced less than $5).

If you invest in the speculative level, try this strategy. Set a limit on the amount you are willing to lose, much like you might on a trip to Las Vegas. Invest that amount. *If you win*, cash out, take your profits and invest them at a less-risky level of the pyramid. Reinvest your original principal in another speculative investment.

If you lose, don't buy any more speculative investments until you earn back what you lost. Then decide if you want to move those earnings into the speculative level again. This way, you will never lose more than you originally committed to speculative investments.

Buy these investments *only* from someone you know and trust, and only after you completely understand the investment. Keep no more than *5 percent* of your investible funds in this level of risk during any financial stage of life.

Summary

Now that you know how the investment pyramid works, how can you use it?

- List everything you own, with its current market value.

19

- Place each item in the appropriate level of the investment pyramid, creating your Personal Pyramid.
- Calculate the subtotal of what you own in each level.
- Calculate the total of all levels combined.
- Calculate the percentage of your total investible funds that are in each level. (Divide level total into pyramid total to calculate the percentage.)
- Always be aware of the risk associated with the level of any promised total return—most conservative, conservative, moderate, aggressive or speculative.
- Complete and analyze your Personal Pyramid on an annual basis so you begin each year's plan with *where you are*. This snapshot (or diagnosis) of your financial condition can be a report card showing your progress each year.

Now you have seen a picture of the puzzle. Let's get out the rest of the pieces and begin to put them together. You have completed the first of the three steps to successful financial decision-making. Now you know *where you are*.

Step 2: Determine Where You Are Going

Now you are ready to take the second of the three steps to successful financial decision-making: You're ready to determine *where you are going*.

The *Goal Pyramid* for your financial stage of life is a guideline for where you are going. The Goal Pyramid shows you a specific percentage of the total that you should own in each level of the pyramid. There is a different Goal Pyramid for each of the four financial stages of life. You can determine which one you are in by reading this chapter.

2. How do I develop a Goal Pyramid?

People ask us every day, "How much money should I have, and how should it be invested?" We like to say it's the stage, not the age. Why? Consider Jim and Sheila. They are both 40 years old and are ready to retire. Their income in the future will come from their investments, no more salaries. Their friends Mike and Julie, who are also 40, have just had their first child. Does each family need the same amount of money invested in the same way? Surely not. Jim and Sheila need a larger portion of their funds invested for income and preservation of principal than Mike and Julie. They will have some funds invested in growth to protect them from inflation. Mike and Julie need a larger proportion invested in growth to deflect the expenses of child-rearing and education, and to protect them from inflation.

People may marry at 20 or 40, have children early or late, and may retire at 50 or 70. These activities are the life criteria for each financial stage of life.

Keep in mind that the proportion of income investments and the proportion of growth investments you should own differ with each financial stage of life. You need to have your money working together, which means more than having your money working for you. It requires having the proper proportion of your funds invested in each of the five levels of the investment pyramid, for your particular financial stage of life.

The four financial stages of life are:

1. Getting started
2. Getting growing
3. Getting comfortable
4. Taking it easy

Stage 1: Getting started

This begins with establishing a career; determining your budget for living and saving; buying furniture and cars; saving for a home; and, most importantly, establishing an emergency fund of six months' living expenses in a highly liquid investment, such as a money market.

In this stage you are building a strong financial base. Generally, you will not have a lot of extra cash after paying living expenses, but it is imperative to start your financial future by earning some interest and making saving a healthy habit. Save what you can, and watch it grow. Your investment outlook for this first stage is long-term.

Stage 2: Getting growing

In this stage you may purchase your first home; establish active investing for the future (including retirement); and accumulate adult "toys" like boats or cars. This stage may also include getting married and raising children (and saving for their education). Such busy lifestyles may require two incomes. Your investment outlook for this stage is also generally long-term.

Stage 3: Getting comfortable

This stage begins after major responsibilities and high living expenses are over. If there were children, they have left the nest and no longer need your support. (If they are **MONEYWISE** they won't!) Now is the time to prepare for retirement by:

- Investing larger amounts of money.
- Making sure your retirement dollars are growing effectively to provide you with adequate support when you need it.

You accept less risk in your Personal Pyramid during this stage because you cannot afford to lose principal. However, you should continue to own some moderate and aggressive-level growth investments to protect yourself against inflation.

Stage 4: Taking it easy

You may be 50, or you may be 70—but it's time for retirement! This stage can last 30 years or more. Often, people say, "I don't need to manage my money; I'm retired." *Wrong!* This may be the longest financial stage of your life. You will need some growth investments during retirement to protect you from inflation. A loaf of bread doesn't cost what it did 30 years ago. What do you think it will cost in 2020? The growth portion of your Personal Pyramid protects your buying power.

Moneywise Tip

Saving for retirement means accumulating buying power rather than accumulating dollars.

If you move into a lower tax bracket in retirement, determine whether you need to convert any lower-earning, tax-exempt investments to higher-earning taxable investments. Remember, it isn't how much you make but how much you *keep* that counts. Maximize your *after-tax income.*

Summary

Now you can see why the Goal Pyramids for Jim and Sheila and Mike and Julie are very different. It makes sense that needs of retirees are very different from needs of new parents—monetary or otherwise.

The following are the Goal Pyramids for each of the four financial stages of life. *These are tools, not rules,* and here are some observations:

- Note how the portion allocated in each level changes as you move through the various stages.

You should have about 70 percent in growth (moderate and aggressive levels of the pyramid, maybe some speculative) during the *getting started* stage of life, and that portion declines to 40 percent in the *taking it easy* stage.

• A variance of 5 percent either way in any level is acceptable.

Once you understand the four financial stages of life, how can you use them?

Determine which stage you are in and note the percentages for each level of your Goal Pyramid. Now you have completed the second of three steps to successful financial decision making. You know *where you are going*.

Goal Pyramids for each of the four financial stages.

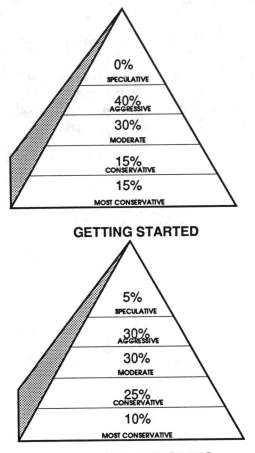

GETTING STARTED

GETTING GROWING

Goal Pyramids for each of the four financial stages.

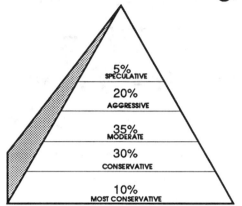

5%
SPECULATIVE

20%
AGGRESSIVE

35%
MODERATE

30%
CONSERVATIVE

10%
MOST CONSERVATIVE

GETTING COMFORTABLE

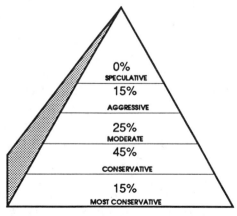

0%
SPECULATIVE

15%
AGGRESSIVE

25%
MODERATE

45%
CONSERVATIVE

15%
MOST CONSERVATIVE

TAKING IT EASY

Chapter 3

Step 3: Plan How to Get There

When you compare your Goal Pyramid to your Personal Pyramid, you will see differences in some levels. Use these differences to decide what to buy in the future. Buy more investments in the levels where your Personal Pyramid contains less than your Goal Pyramid.

Let's apply the concept of *where you are* and *where you are going* to Jane's Personal Pyramid, using the diagram showing the three steps to successful financial decision-making on page 31. Jane has $50,000 of investible funds. She has made a list of everything she owns (except her primary home and personal items not for sale), assigned each item to its level in the pyramid, totaled the dollar amount in each level, and divided it by $50,000 to arrive at the percentage invested in each level.

This is a partial picture of how she is diversified. Jane's Personal Pyramid is 2 percent speculative, 25 percent aggressive, 50 percent moderate, 5 percent conservative, 18 percent most conservative. Preparing this pyramid is the first step.

Let's take Step 2. Jane determines which of the four financial stages of life she is in, and inserts the Goal Pyramid for that stage in *where you are going*. Jane is in the "getting started" stage of life and the appropriate percentages to own in each level are shown in the illustration on page 31. I'm sure you've heard the saying, "If you don't know where you are going, any road will take you there." It was never more true than with money.

Now, and only now is Jane ready for Step 3, which is *how to get there*. How to get there means buying or selling *any* investment...CD, mutual fund, stock or bond.

Jane can compare her Personal Pyramid at each level to her Goal Pyramid and see where she needs to make changes. (Keep in mind, if the amount Jane owns in any level is within 5 percent of the Goal Pyramid, it's OK.) Will she need more speculative? No. She's within the advised 5-percent variance. So put "no change" next to the speculative level on the Goal Pyramid.

Aggressive? She needs more, so she will put a plus sign next to that level. She wants to increase from 25 percent to 40 percent in order to reach her goal.

Moderate? Oops! She has 50 percent compared to the guideline of 30 percent. Write a minus sign in the line next to moderate.

Conservative? Oops again. She has 5 percent rather than the suggested 15 percent. Write a plus sign next to conservative.

Most conservative? Jane has 18 percent, well within the 5-percent variance allowed by the guidelines. Put "no change" next to most conservative.

Here's how Jane uses this valuable information. *The next time she has money to invest*, such as an IRA contribution, before April 15, what will be the level in the pyramid of the investment she will buy? Conservative or aggressive.

Now, and only now, Jane is ready to talk with a financial advisor, because she will need current examples of conservative and aggressive investments to buy that will bring her Personal Pyramid into line with her Goal Pyramid.

If she were called by a broker and asked to buy the latest "good investment," a blue chip stock such as AT&T, which is in the moderate level, what would she say? No. Because she already owns enough in the moderate level. Using her Personal Pyramid, she can tell the difference between a good investment—and a good investment for *her*...and so can you.

Should Jane immediately sell investments she owns in the moderate level because she has too large a proportion there? No. She will make changes in those investments as they mature or when they give her other reasons to sell, such as poor performance compared to their investment objective. Also, note that the proportion Jane owns in each of these levels will decrease as she adds to the other levels. This result is a function of the arithmetic—no magic here.

How do you invest to create your ideal Personal Pyramid? Once you decide whether you need aggressive, moderate, conservative and/or most conservative investments, you will need to know how to select them. That's what you will learn in Chapters 4 through 15. Here are some tips to help you.

- Make the commitment to buy investments that fill the gaps between your Personal Pyramid and your Goal Pyramid the next time you have money to invest.

- *Do not* sell everything at once and buy all new investments. Some people are advised to do so by unethical advisors who want to generate commissions. No one's Personal Pyramid is so bad that they need to sell everything and start over.

THREE STEPS TO SUCCESSFUL DECISION MAKING

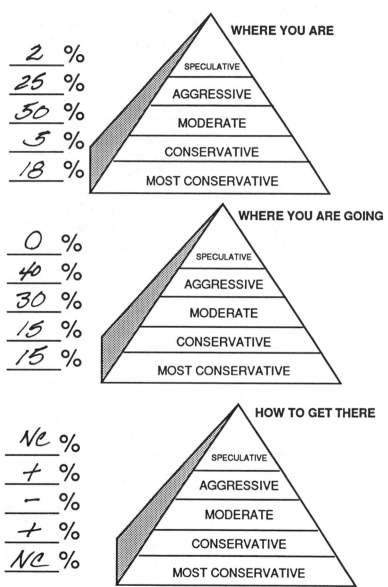

WHERE YOU ARE

2 %
25 %
50 %
5 %
18 %

SPECULATIVE
AGGRESSIVE
MODERATE
CONSERVATIVE
MOST CONSERVATIVE

WHERE YOU ARE GOING

0 %
40 %
30 %
15 %
15 %

SPECULATIVE
AGGRESSIVE
MODERATE
CONSERVATIVE
MOST CONSERVATIVE

HOW TO GET THERE

NC %
+ %
– %
+ %
NC %

SPECULATIVE
AGGRESSIVE
MODERATE
CONSERVATIVE
MOST CONSERVATIVE

31

- Evaluate what you own and how your investments are performing for you. If you are pleased with your investments, keep them. If you are not, plan to sell them and buy investments in the levels of your Personal Pyramid where you have gaps.

Summary

Remember the story of the broker who calls at 6:30 p.m., asking you to buy some stock? What should he have asked first? "Where are you?" And "Where are you going?" The investment might be good for you—or only good for generating a commission for the salesperson. First, find out in which level of the pyramid the investment belongs. Then ask yourself, "Would an addition to my Personal Pyramid in that level bring it more in line with my goal?" Remember, it might be a good investment, but to be a good investment *for you*, it must fill a gap in your Personal Pyramid.

There you have it. Three steps to successful financial decision-making. Use them wisely. You can do it!

Chapter 4

Questions to Ask Before You *Buy* Any Investment

Would you spend an hour to make $1,000? That's what you do when you take time to learn about an investment.

When you go into a dealership to buy a car, you have a mental list of what you want:

Van, station wagon, sedan, convertible; Automatic transmission or manual; Two door or four door; Miles per gallon, etc.

You have a favorite color in mind, but you want the hard facts first, right? If you want a red convertible and they show you a red van, it's a waste of time at best and insulting at worst. Consider your financial conversation in the same manner. Many advisors sell the "color" before they talk about the features: "This is a great investment—it will double in six months." Insist upon getting the "miles per gallon" or, historic and projected total return, how and when the investment makes money, and why it is expected to continue in the future, before you listen to the "color."

Moneywise Tip

You wouldn't buy a car you couldn't drive. Don't buy an investment you don't understand.

Here are seven questions you can ask (and answer) in less than an hour to help you preserve your money and make it grow carefully. Ask these questions before you invest any money *and* also ask the questions from the chapters that follow, about the specific types of investment (stock, bond, etc.).

3. How does this investment make its money?

- *How do I make money by owning it?* (The first thing you need to know about an investment is how it works—how it makes money and why it has value.)

- *If the investment is a common stock, what product or service does the company offer?* (When we were stockbrokers, occasionally people would call to buy a stock when all they knew was the stock symbol— they did not know the name of the company or what the company sells to make money.)

Moneywise Tip

Buying on a "hot tip" without sound facts about a company is like buying a house you haven't seen in an unknown city. That house could have a hole in the roof or a crack in the foundation! Keep asking questions. It's your money.

- *Does the company produce something of value?*
- *Does it have a market niche or a special way of doing something ordinary?*
- *Does it produce something that creates customer loyalty?*
- *Is the company making a profit?*
- *Has it done so consistently?*
- *Are sales and profits growing?* (Check *net earnings* and *earnings per share.* They should have a positive year-to-year trend for the past five years.)

Start-up companies (initial public offerings, or IPOs) with little or no profit, generally belong in the speculative level of the investment pyramid.

If the investment is a bond or limited partnership, ask "Will it actually return money to me; or do my benefits come in other forms, such as promised tax savings?"

Municipal bonds, for example, pay interest that is exempt from taxation by one or more of the federal, state or local governments. Many limited partnerships were created to lose money, thereby generating tax losses for the investor. These were very popular tax shelters before tax laws changed to prohibit passive losses as a reduction of ordinary income. Those who owned partnerships during the period in which the laws changed found that once-valuable investments quickly became worthless.

4. When will my original investment (principal) be returned?

Now you know how an investment can make you money, but it is equally important to find out before you invest how to get your money back. It is usually easier to play the game knowing all the rules ahead of time.

Keep asking questions.

- *Does this investment have a set date upon which my funds will be returned to me?*
- *Is there any guarantee that the amount returned will be the same or greater than the amount originally invested?*
- *Will I suffer a penalty for requesting the return of my principal before the maturity date?*
- *If there is not a set maturity, how difficult is it to liquidate (sell) my investment?*
- *Will it take minutes, hours, days, weeks or months?*
- *Will I lose money if I must sell quickly?*

For example: Advertisements for Certificates of Deposit (CDs) state "substantial penalty for early withdrawal" so you know the rules before you invest. You will pay a penalty to get your money back early.

Mutual funds, on the other hand, have no maturity dates. You can liquidate your shares at any time. However, there is no guarantee that they will be worth the amount you originally invested. For example, growth mutual funds, which invest in growth stocks, change in value every day based on the changing prices of the individual stocks owned by the fund. Due to price volatility, we recommend you plan to own the fund for at least three years in order to enhance your chance of earning the expected total return. Chapter 7 gives you more questions to ask about mutual funds.

Knowing when and how your original principal will be returned is a comforting feeling. Finding out up front could make a difference in your investment decision. Keep in mind, as you keep asking more questions, you are gathering data for an important decision. The more data you gather, the more informed your decision will be.

5. What earnings will I receive from this investment, when, and how?

All investments work differently. If you choose an investment for income purposes, find out when and how often you will receive a check. There is nothing worse than hearing, "Your interest is paid every six months," when you were expecting a monthly check. The following questions will help.

- *Will I make money through capital appreciation, interest, dividends or a combination of these?*
- *When will payments be made—monthly, quarterly or semi-annually?*
- *Will I receive capital appreciation, during the life of the investment or only when I sell or it matures?*
- *If there are dividends, can they be reinvested?*
- *Is there a charge or commission for reinvesting dividends or income?*
- *Is the level of earnings guaranteed (such as with a bond) or can it vary (as with a stock)?*

For example, most corporate bonds pay interest semi-annually at the coupon rate. This means a $1,000 par value (face value). Anheuser Busch 9 percent bond pays $90 per year in two installments of $45.

Zero coupon bonds, on the other hand, pay all interest at maturity. There are no interim interest payments. The interest is implied in the difference between purchase price and the maturity value. For example, a zero coupon bond yielding 8 percent and maturing in 10 years at $1,000 costs $450. The difference between your purchase price and the maturity value ($1,000 - $450 = $550) is your interest.

Keep good records if you receive interest or dividends from your investments. Also, it might be helpful to mark on a calendar when your payments are due. That way you should have fewer surprises.

6. Which of the five levels of the investment pyramid does this represent?

Before making any purchase decision, consider how an additional investment in any level affects your pyramid. If it will not fill a gap, consider another investment.

Remember Jane's Personal Pyramid? When she was asked to buy a moderate-level blue chip stock, it might have been a good investment, but *not a good investment for her*.

7. Where is the risk?

- *What is the nature of the risk?*
- *Is there inflation risk?*

- *Interest rate risk (value risk or reinvestment rate risk)?*
- *Business risk?*
- *Market risk?*
- *Liquidity risk?*

All investments have risk—even cash has risk. It is important to have a variety of investments so you don't have too much of the same type of risk. Don't put all your eggs in one basket, even if you plan to watch that basket carefully. The real estate moguls in the 1980s endured huge losses in the 1990s, partially because they did not diversify their risk with different types of investments to sustain them through economic cycles in real estate.

Inflation risk is what we experience with our daily purchases. Will a dollar's worth of goods today be worth the same five years from now; or, will the dollars returned from an investment buy less than the dollars invested? How many loaves of bread can you buy today with $1? Currently, one (maybe, with a coupon); in 1970, about three; in 1950, about six; in 1940, about 10.

You face inflation risk with any investment that pays back a fixed dollar amount in the future, with no chance of growth in principal. These investments include CDs, bonds, money market accounts and fixed annuities.

In contrast, the value of hard assets, such as real estate, collectibles and precious metals generally rises with inflation. Common stocks have the potential for growth of principal. This growth in principal can offset the loss in purchasing power of the dollar.

Look at the following inflation table. During the last 20 years, the rate of inflation has averaged 6 percent. If inflation continues to average 6 percent, $1 will be worth only 31 cents in 20 years.

What Will $1.00 Be Worth?

			Inflation Rate				
YR	3%	5%	6%	8%	10%	15%	20%
5	$.86	$.78	$.75	$.68	$.62	$.50	$.40
6	.84	.75	.70	.63	.56	.43	.33
7	.81	.71	.65	.58	.51	.38	.28
8	.79	.68	.63	.54	.47	.33	.23
9	.77	.64	.59	.50	.42	.28	.19
10	.74	.61	.56	.46	.39	.25	.16
15	.64	.48	.42	.32	.24	.12	.06
20	.55	.38	.31	.21	.15	.06	.03
25	.48	.30	.23	.15	.09	.03	.01
30	.41	.23	.17	.10	.06	.02	
35	.36	.18	.13	.07	.04	.01	
40	.31	.14	.10	.05	.02		
45	.26	.11	.07	.03	.01		
50	.23	.09	.05	.02	.01		

Interest rate risk generally applies to bonds or CDs and can be divided into two categories: value and reinvestment rate risk.

Value risk results from the fact that when interest rates rise, bond prices fall, and vice versa. So, if you own a bond and general interest rates rise, the market value (the price you receive if you sell) falls. Why?

Let's say you buy a $1,000 bond today that pays 8 percent, and you hold it for a year. This time next year you would like to sell your bond and Joe Smith is in the market to buy one. However, general interest rates have risen to 9 percent. Joe can either buy a new bond that pays 9 percent, or buy yours, which pays 8 percent. What will you do to entice him to buy your 8-percent bond? Lower the price.

Hence, as general interest rates rise, the prices of existing bonds fall. On the other hand, if you were holding the 8-percent bond and current bonds available were yielding 7 percent, Joe would be willing to pay more than $1,000 for the bond.

What should you do if your bond loses value when market rates change? *Do not sell.* After all, you bought the bond for fixed income, not capital appreciation. If you still expect to receive the full face value at maturity, there is little reason to take a loss now. You're affected by value risk only in the event that you *need* to sell before maturity, in which case you could lose principal when you sell your bond.

Reinvestment rate risk is the risk that, if interest rates fall after you make an investment, you will be reinvesting the interest payments you receive at a lower rate. It also means that when the investment matures, or if it is called before maturity, your choices for reinvesting the principal (in the same level of risk on your Personal Pyramid) could result in your earning a lower rate of interest. In times of falling interest rates, this can be especially hazardous to anyone living on income from a portfolio of bonds or CDs.

41

Especially vulnerable to reinvestment rate risk are *callable bonds*, those the issuer has the right to "call away" from you, and return your principal before maturity. Issuers will do this when interest rates fall because they can issue new bonds and pay a lower rate, just as you would when refinancing your home. While this is good for the issuer, you have your principal returned unexpectedly and are forced to accept a lower rate of return when you re-invest it in the same level of your Personal Pyramid.

Business risk is encountered in common stocks as well as corporate and municipal bonds. This is the risk of problems in a corporation or institution that could cause earnings to fall adversely affecting stock price or threatening its ability to make interest of principal payments on a bond. Possibilities include management errors, faulty products, increased competition, changing consumer tastes, etc.

BUSINESS RISK

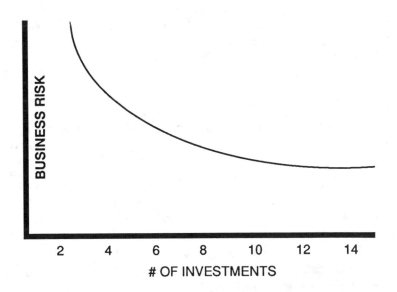

The most extreme result of business risk is bankruptcy. If you hold a company's common stock, you are at the bottom of the list (behind the lawyers, the Internal Revenue Service, the banks, bondholders and preferred stockholders) when it comes to getting any money back.

You can minimize business risk by practicing the principle of diversification. When you own stocks of individual companies, collect 15 or more different stocks in different industries. Experts say that the business risk of any one company is eliminated when you have 14 others.

MARKET RISK

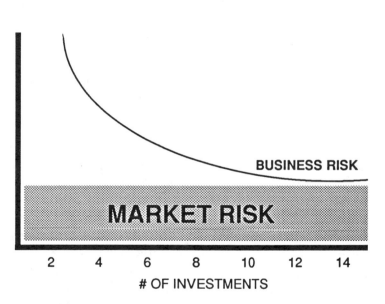

You can minimize business risk by practicing the principle of diversification.

Market risk is the type of risk that remains in a diversified portfolio of 15 stocks. It's the risk that the market, or economy as a whole, performs poorly, causing stocks and bonds to change in value, regardless of the fundamentals of the individual companies they represent. An example is the stock market crash of '87. Market risk will affect virtually all investments and cannot be controlled by the investor. You can minimize the effect of market risk somewhat by holding investments that are expected to behave differently from each other under changing economic conditions. This is why it is especially important to own combinations of stocks, bonds, real estate and cash.

Moneywise Tip

*The **Rule of Five** predicts that for every five stocks you purchase, three will perform as expected, one will have stellar performance, and one will be your worst nightmare. Choose all five and your total return will average close to the middle of the road. Choose one and it could be the nightmare.*

Liquidity risk is the risk that you cannot sell an investment quickly without losing principal. You can sell your house tomorrow but probably not at your asking price. Liquidity risk affects those investments that do not have active secondary markets, and investments that are in very volatile or cyclical markets, such as real estate.

These are the five types of risk. When you have identified the types that apply to the investment you are considering, ask yourself whether your other holdings are exposed to the same risks. Again, diversification is the key to protecting your prin-cipal, and making it grow.

---

8. Is this taxable, tax-exempt, or tax-deferred, and do special conditions apply?

- *Are there any IRS penalties for early withdrawal, such as with an annuity?*

- *Is it federally, state, locally taxable?*
- *How does its tax status affect its actual real return?*

For example, compare a 6.5-percent municipal bond issued in your state to a 9-percent corporate bond. Which one would you prefer to own? If your answer is, "It depends on my tax bracket," you are correct. Assume a 28-percent federal tax bracket and a 6-percent state tax rate for the following example:

	6.5% Municipal Bond	9% Corporate Bond
Annual interest	$65.00	$90.00
Less federal taxes at 28%	$0	$25.20
Less state taxes at 6%	$0	$5.40
The money you keep	$65.00	$59.40

Moneywise Tip

Forget the fancy formulas, just determine how much money you keep. Whenever you compare two or more investments that are taxed differently, always compare on an after-tax basis.

The corporate bond loses 28 percent of its yield to federal taxes and 6 percent of its yield to state taxes, leaving a real return of only 5.9 percent. The interest from the municipal bond is not federally taxable and, because it was issued in your state, will not be subject to state taxes. For you, the municipal bond is better.

Taxes are very important. However, don't let them scare you away from buying or selling an investment. You can see from the example that what you need to know is how much money you keep. To do this, take the taxes out and see what you have left. Only then will you have the right information to decide if an investment is good for you.

9. How does the seller of this investment make money when I purchase and/or own this investment?

- *Is the seller the only one who makes money?* (If you haven't asked the other questions in this chapter, he or she may be.)

- *Does the seller or broker recommending the investment earn a commission?* (There isn't anything wrong with the broker earning a commission; that's how he or she makes a living and how you pay for the help you receive. However, make sure that the commission or other fees paid to the seller aren't excessive.)

Moneywise Tip

You don't have to pay the most to get the best.

If anyone tells you he or she is selling totally commission-free, be cautious—about the seller/broker and about the investment. Ask how he or she makes money. *There is no free lunch. You wouldn't work for free either.*

Example 1: When you buy a "load" mutual fund, the sales agent receives the "load" or commission for helping you choose the fund. The mutual fund company receives an annual management fee for its work. Both of these fees should be disclosed in the prospectus. Both should be reasonable when compared to funds with a similar investment objective. You can use the *Morningstar Mutual Funds* report to compare features and results of mutual funds. This report is available in most libraries or you can order a subscription.

Example 2: When you purchase bonds, the commission is built into the price you pay for the bond. You will rarely see a separate line item for commission. That doesn't mean you don't pay one; it means that the price quoted to you *includes* the mark-up. Just as a clothing store marks up its merchandise before selling to the consumer, a brokerage firm adds a mark-up to its bonds.

Example 3: When you purchase stock or options, the commissions charged can vary greatly, depending upon the firm and the type of service you need. If you need research and advice, use a full-service firm. If you don't need research and advice, don't pay for them; use a discount firm to place your transaction. The execution of your trades, or how fast your order hits the market, should be the same with both types of brokers.

Fees will vary among full-service firms and also among discount firms, so compare often. Also, if you trade often or in large amounts within a firm, ask that your commissions be reduced.

Example 4: Insurance companies pay commissions and other compensation to their brokers and agents from their earnings on your premiums, so you have every right to know what your agent is paid on your transaction. Sellers of annuities can earn as much as 8 percent—we believe 4 to 5 percent is fair. Sellers of cash value (permanent) life insurance policies (see Chapter 12) are paid up to 100 percent of your first year premiums—we believe 50 percent or less is fair.

Summary

Make sure you have good answers to each of the "Questions to Ask Before You Buy." Put all of your information together and look at it carefully before you make an investment decision. You can see why it is impossible to give an immediate answer to the broker who called at 6:30 p.m. Getting the answers to these questions may take you an hour or several days. Don't feel pressured. If an investment is that good today, it should be just as good tomorrow or the next day.

Chapter 5

Questions to Ask Before You *Sell* Any Investment

Even for experienced investors, knowing when to sell can be twice as hard as knowing when to buy. It is easy to become attached to your investments—you were careful selecting and watching them, now it could be time to cut the ropes and let go. How do you know when to do it? Be sure to ask these questions before you sell.

10. Have my investment objectives changed?

What were my investment objectives at the time of purchase? Preservation of principal? Income? Growth? Growth and income? Aggressive growth? International diversification or speculation?

Has my objective for tax-exempt or tax-deferred income changed?

With every change in income tax brackets, the relative attractiveness of tax-exempt investments will change. Moving into lower tax brackets during retirement may reduce your desire to hold tax-exempt or tax-deferred investments. As the tax deferral's relative value decreases, you may not be willing to pay the fees associated with these products.

Am I moving into another of the four financial stages of life?

Your Personal Pyramid works most effectively when you have the proper proportion of your funds in each of the five levels of the pyramid, for your financial stage of life. Chapter 2 gives a complete explanation.

11. Do I have a better opportunity for the proceeds?

Have I identified another investment that would better fit my needs?

An investment doesn't have to be "bad" to cause you to sell it. You may have found another one that better suits your needs and objectives.

Is there an investment available that would give me a higher total return without exposing me to more risk?

When you are analyzing alternative investments, be sure to consider how they fit your Personal Pyramid. The expected return on an aggressive stock will be higher than on a CD, but the risk is also higher. Compare total returns only on investments with similar risk levels.

If the investment is not performing poorly, hold onto it, even while you are considering others. Always keep your money working for you.

---

12. Am I sufficiently diversified?

As we said earlier, never put all your eggs in one basket, even if it seems like a great basket. One of the biggest mistakes people make is to rely on one or two large investments. Diversification is the key to successful investing. One issue of diversification arises when someone earns a salary from the same company that funds his or her benefits (retirement and other compensation) *with company stock.* There is reason for caution here. Consider the risk of losing your job at a time when the company's stock is at a low point. If you are in this situation and your company plan allows the choice, consider changing a portion of your investible funds from company stock to a moderate-growth mutual fund within your 401(k) or pension plan. Another alternative is to consider selling a portion of the stock or exercising some stock options (in "after-tax" plans only), and diversifying with the proceeds.

Business owners who have a substantial portion of their net worth invested in their own company incur this same risk. We suggest they begin a company retirement plan and invest those funds in something unrelated to the business. Any business or self-employed person can establish a Simplified Employee Pension Plan (SEP). Each year, you may contribute up to the lesser of 15 percent of compensation or $30,000.[2] Ask your tax advisor about the specifics.

Complete diversification is achieved by diversifying in three ways: length of maturity, type of risk incurred and type of investment within each level. Keep this in mind as you read the following chapters.

---

[2] Details will vary as tax laws change. The principal of tax-deferred growth is what is important here.

13. Has this investment lagged behind its competitors and the market averages?

The only way to tell if you are getting a fair total return on an investment is to periodically compare your returns to those of investments with similar objectives, and to the market averages.

For stocks and stock mutual funds, compare with the *Standard & Poor's Composite Index of 500 Stocks (S&P 500)*, an index of 500 stocks whose performance is used as a benchmark for the stock market.

For individual stocks, compare price performance to other stocks in the same industry, using the industry reports in *Value Line Investment Survey*.[3] Read those industry reports to compare the industry's performance to others and to learn about its future prospects.

For mutual funds, compare individual funds to others with the same investment objective, using the rating system available in *Morningstar Mutual Funds*, or the rankings in any of the financial magazines.

For bonds, periodically check the company's rating by Standard & Poor's or Moody's. Changes in these ratings, the highest of which are AAA or Aaa, can signal changes in the quality of your bond.

Continued underperformance can signal poor management or perhaps just a poor investment. If your investment underperforms—*sell it.*

---

[3] *Value Line Investment Survey* is generally available in the reference room of your library, from your financial advisor or by subscription.

14. Are economic conditions poor for this type of investment?

Is the economy in a recession?

Recessions create mixed signals for the stock market and may affect individual stocks differently. In general, stock prices rise when interest rates fall, because investors seeking higher returns move funds from banks and money market funds into the stock market. However, if corporate profits fall during a recession, and prospects for growth are dampened, stock prices can lose ground.

Defensive stocks, those in industries such as food, beverages or household products, generally hold their ground in recessionary times. Consumers with reduced incomes continue to purchase the products that these companies produce. **Cyclical stocks**, such as auto manufacturers or home building companies, are often hurt the most in a recession.

A recession is often bad for real estate, which can serve as a hedge against inflation. As inflation drops there is less incentive to invest in real estate. When disposable income decreases for individuals, the demand for, and thus prices of, residential real estate can drop. Furthermore, falling profits in the corporate world decrease the demand for commercial real estate. You may remember what happened to Houston when the oil business declined.

Recessionary times usually result in higher bond prices. Why? In a recession, interest rates generally fall, causing the prices of existing bonds to rise.

Is the economy in a boom?

Unload defensive stocks in favor of cyclical stocks, which will benefit from a strong economy. Consider selling bond funds if interest rates are on the rise.[4] If they are heavily invested in long-term bonds, their net asset value will decline as the prices of those bonds fall. Keep individual bonds with good credit ratings. As long as you hold to maturity, you will receive the face value of the bond. There is no reason to sell before maturity and take a loss in principal.

If you are searching for income and capital preservation in a rising interest-rate environment, consider money markets or adjustable-rate, short-term-bond funds. Both are designed to maintain a constant net asset value while their interest rates fluctuate.

Has there been a scandal in a particular industry or with a specific type of financial product?

We all remember the scandals related to junk bond markets and the huge losses they created for many bond-holders. Since the height of the publicity about Michael Milken and the millions of dollars lost by the savings and loan industry, junk bond prices have been creeping back.

When something like the crash of '87 happens, go back to your original objectives—the reasons why you bought the investment. If your objectives were long-term and you see little change in the fundamentals of the investment, do not rush to sell just because the price has dropped. Make a slow and sound decision, not a quick one.

15. Has management changed?

Management changes can have a positive or negative effect on a stock or mutual fund. However, they create

---

[4] In general, we recommend owning individual bonds rather than bond funds. See Chapter 9 for a complete explanation.

uncertainty, which can cause price volatility. Be cautious when a company does not have anyone groomed to succeed the chief executive officer. Be careful when a mutual fund changes managers; the past performance of the fund may no longer be a good way to judge possible future performance.

---

16. Have I become emotionally attached to a loser?

It is easy to become personally involved with your investments, especially if you choose them with as much care as we recommend. Not only does holding on to a losing stock cost you money, it may keep you from buying a winner.

Moneywise Tip

Avoid confusing sentiment with profitability.

Summary

It is much easier to learn about buying investments than it is to learn when to sell them. However, the seven questions in this chapter should get you started. Experience will help, and so may the following thoughts:

- Never make a sell decision based on tax implications. Sell investments based on their fundamentals; their performance and prospects for the future. If you avoid selling because you will pay taxes on the gains, you may end up with an investment that declines to the point that you no longer have any gains.

- No one ever went broke taking a profit. Don't chastise yourself too much for selling an investment that continues to rise after you no longer own it. If your reasons for selling were well-founded, you may just be ahead of the pack. Occasionally, investors follow this axiom too closely. They should consider the next one.

- Don't pick the flowers and keep the weeds. If you sell investments that reach your profit expectations and hold those that don't, you may end up with a portfolio of poor performers after you sell all your winners. Base your sell decisions on the seven questions and you'll end up holding some winners past your original profit expectations and getting rid of some of your losers.

- You must only be right more than *half* of the time in order to make a profit. Cut your losses quickly and learn from your mistakes. Investing is not an exact science.

Chapter 6

Questions to Ask About Your Pension, 401(k) or IRA

17. What are IRAs and 401(k)s?

An IRA is an Individual Retirement Account, defined by the IRS to help individuals save for retirement. You may benefit from an IRA in two ways:

1. All IRAs enjoy tax deferral of earnings. In other words, you don't pay taxes on any dividends, interest or capital gains earned on the investment until they are withdrawn from the account.

2. IRA contributions may be tax-deductible against ordinary income, depending on your level of income and employer-provided retirement plans. Check with your tax advisor.

A 401(k) plan, provided by an employer, is a retirement plan that allows pre-tax contributions to an account in your name, and enjoys the same tax-deferral on earnings as IRAs. Additionally, many employers match employee contributions with cash or company stock.

18. How much should I contribute to my 401(k) or IRA?

Contribute the maximum that you can afford, within the legal limits (See Question 23). Revise your budget to do so, if necessary. Retirement plans such as IRAs and company 401(k)s are two of the few remaining tax breaks we receive from the federal government. Your return on the first day is 28 percent if you are in the 28-percent tax bracket! For example, when you contribute $2,000, you have saved yourself $560 in federal taxes. ($560 ÷ 2000 = 28%) How many of us would jump at an investment with a 28-percent total return with no risk? Consider various state and local income taxes and it becomes even more appealing.

Moneywise Tip

It's not the money you make that counts, it's the money you keep.

Eventually you will have to pay taxes on that income. No problem. Let's compare saving $2,000 after taxes ($1,440 in a 28-percent tax bracket) in a non-IRA account to saving $2,000 pre-tax in an IRA. Both investments earn income at 8 percent for 20 years. The entire amount of the IRA investment is taxed upon withdrawal. The 8-percent income for the non-IRA is taxed annually.

One-time investment Earns 8% annually	Non - IRA/401k investment	IRA/401k investment
Money available to invest	$2,000	$2,000
Taxes paid before investing	$560	$0
After-tax investment	$1,440	$2,000
Value after 20 years (non-IRA income taxed annually at 28%)	$4,414	$9,322
28% tax upon withdrawal	$0	$2,610
The money you keep after 20 years	$4,414	$6,712

99 Great Answers to Investment Questions

Now let's see how it works if you invest that money every year for 20 years:

Annual investment for each of 20 years. Earns 8% annually	Non - IRA/401k investment	IRA/401k investment
Money available to invest	$2,000	$2,000
Taxes paid before investing	$560	$0
Annual after-tax investment	$1,440	$2,000
Value after 20 years (non-IRA income taxed annually at 28%)	$51,625	$91,524
28% tax upon withdrawal	$0	$25,627
The money you keep after 20 years	$51,625	$65,897

One-time investment Earns 8% annually	Non - 401k investment	401k investment
Money available to invest	$2,000	$2,000
Taxes paid before investing	$560	$0
After-tax investment	$1,440	$2,000
Matching funds provided by employer	$0	$1,000
Total initial investment	$1,440	$3,000
Value after 20 years (non-IRA income taxed annually at 28%)	$4,414	$13,983
28% tax upon withdrawal	$0	$3,915
The money you keep after 20 years	$4,414	$10,068

What about 401(k) plans offered by your employer? They may be an even *better* way to save, because many companies offer matching programs that match up to 100 percent of the employee contributions. How much do you keep with the same $2,000 investment in a company plan that matches 50 percent of employee contributions? Review the chart on the previous page:

19. If I invest in a 401(k) or an IRA, when can I withdraw the money without penalty?

Plan to begin after age 59½ and before age 70½. Before age 59½, withdrawals are subject to a 10-percent penalty by the IRS and the full value of the withdrawal is added to your taxable income for the year. (Check with your tax advisor for hardship exceptions.) After age 59½, you *may* withdraw your money without penalty and after age 70½, you *must* begin withdrawals. After age 70½, minimum withdrawals are computed by using an IRS actuarial factor, which attempts to evenly divide the value of your IRAs by your estimated remaining years of life.

20. If I leave my job and receive a distribution from my 401(k), what should I do with it?

If you are under age 59½, you must transfer or roll over the money into an IRA to avoid the penalties associated with early withdrawal. The process starts with your naming a new custodian for your IRA account. If your employer will transfer all the assets, as is, to the new custodian, it is a transfer.

If their plan does not allow a transfer, it will be a rollover, which means the funds pass through your hands rather than from the present custodian to the new custodian. It is less complicated than it appears. Only the paperwork makes the process intimidating. Think of it as moving your furniture (401(k) funds) to a new home address (custodian). You do not necessarily have to sell the old and buy all new. You just need to move everything.

You have 60 days to complete a rollover to a new custodian from the day you *receive* the check or stock. While the 60-day period officially begins when you receive your distribution, unless the item is sent registered, it is often hard to prove. To save yourself any hassle, complete your rollover within 60 days of the date on the check or envelope postmark and copy all dated documents for your files.

You may roll over into an existing IRA or create a new one. If you do roll over into an existing IRA that contains previous contributions, this is called commingling. Doing this prevents you from being able to roll those funds into your next employer's retirement plan, which may or may not be desirable.

Should I choose a rollover or a transfer if I plan to reinvest the money in an IRA?

The 1993 tax laws[5] make a transfer much more attractive. The new law dictates that unless the employer completes the distribution with a direct transfer, the employer must withhold 20 percent of the funds for possible tax obligations. You can get that 20 percent back from the IRS at tax time next year if you roll over the full amount of the distribution, but here's the catch—when you roll over the full amount, you must make up the 20 percent withheld with your own money from other sources in order to avoid penalties.

---

[5] Check current laws with your tax advisor.

Example: Kris has left her job and has $40,000 in her company 401(k) plan. She hasn't yet decided how to invest the money, and thus doesn't give her former employer instructions for a transfer of the funds. One day she receives a check in the mail. The check is for $32,000, which is $40,000 value of the account less 20 percent withholding that has been sent to the IRS. To avoid taxes and penalties, she must roll over $40,000 (making up the $8,000 difference herself) into an IRA within 60 days. Then she can file to get the $8,000 back next April. If she only deposits the $32,000 into the IRA, she'll owe a 10-percent penalty plus current income taxes on the $8,000.

21. Do I have to invest a rollover or transfer immediately?

You do not have to make all your *investment decisions* quickly, only your *custodial decision*. You can deposit your distribution, stock or cash into a "self-directed" IRA[6] with a new custodian. It is not necessary to sell the stock, it may be deposited as is. While you are evaluating your Personal Pyramid, ask for any cash received to be invested in the new custodian's money market account. Make your remaining investment decisions later. Once you have named the new custodian by depositing into the IRA, you have met the 60-day rollover deadline.

What if I receive stock from my company plan? Can I roll over part of the money and keep part of it? If I do what happens?

---

[6] A self-directed IRA account allows you to buy stock, mutual funds, bonds, etc., within one IRA.

If you choose to transfer or roll over only part of your distribution, you pay taxes and penalty only on the amount *not* transferred or rolled over.

22. How many rollovers can I have per year?

You can roll the *same* money over once per year. It is possible to have more than one rollover if you have more than one account.

For example, you could receive a distribution from a former employer and roll it into another IRA and, in the same year, take a rollover from a contributory IRA (established outside of your employer, with yearly contributions) and deposit it into another account.

23. Is there a maximum amount that I can roll over or contribute?

You can roll over your entire distribution into another IRA. The maximum that you may contribute annually to an IRA is the lesser of $2,000 or your earned income. A non-working spouse can contribute $250. Your contribution may be deductible from ordinary income on your income taxes depending on your level of income and whether you have any plans available through your employer.

In 1993, the maximum an employee can contribute to a 401(k) is $8,994. Check with your tax advisor for future limits.

24. What is an SEP?

An SEP is a Simplified Employee Pension Plan. Almost any business or self-employed person may establish an SEP. Under current IRS rules, you may contribute up to the lesser of 15 percent of your compensation or $30,000. With an SEP, you are not obligated to make contributions in a given year and you may change the percentage contributed from year to year. You must contribute the same percentage of compensation to all eligible employees.

25. How should I invest the IRA?

Begin by comparing your Personal Pyramid to the Goal Pyramid for your stage of life. As discussed in Chapter 3, your IRA investments should work with your other investible funds to complete your Personal Pyramid. Identify any gaps and make adjustments accordingly. Growth investments should be placed in tax-deferred accounts, such as IRAs, so that capital gains may be taken and taxes avoided until withdrawal from the account.

26. Should I invest my rollover distribution into an annuity?

No. The main reason people invest in annuities is to obtain the tax-deferred status of all income and growth. In other words, an annuity is designed to defer taxes until you cash it in or start to receive income. Your rollover distribution is already eligible for tax protection because it originated in such an account. It is not necessary for you to choose an investment specifically to give you that tax advantage. *You could be paying twice as much in fees, commissions, etc., for the same benefit.*

Summary

A retirement plan is one of the few tax breaks we have left. Through either an IRA, SEP-IRA, or company 401(k), you can make pre-tax contributions to your retirement. In the 28-percent tax bracket, your immediate return is 28 percent in taxes that you don't pay now. Additionally, all investments within a retirement account earn interest, dividends and capital gains without being taxed until withdrawal.

Remember the 10-percent penalty for withdrawal before age 59½ and the fact that you will pay taxes when you withdraw the money. Still, retirement accounts are one of the best ways to make sure you have enough money to retire comfortably. Pay yourself first to save!

Chapter 7

Questions to Ask About Mutual Funds

27. What are mutual funds and what are their advantages?

A mutual fund is a pool of investments managed by an investment company. These companies create and manage large portfolios of different securities, then sell pieces (shares) of these portfolios to the public. Through the purchase of mutual fund shares, an individual can own a portion of a professionally managed, diversified investment portfolio. Decisions such as which securities to buy, hold or sell are delegated to the fund's professional money managers. With today's marketplace getting more and more complex, mutual funds offer a simple, convenient and time-efficient method of investing.

The mutual fund pools money from many investors who have similar objectives. The professional money managers then make investment decisions designed to meet the stated objectives of that particular portfolio or fund. Each share of the fund represents ownership in all of the fund's underlying securities. Dividends and capital gains that are produced by the portfolio are paid out to investors, based upon how many shares they own. In other words, shareholders who invest a few thousand dollars receive the same investment return per dollar as the shareholders who invest hundreds of thousands.

Advantages of owning mutual funds

1. Professional management. Professional money management has long been available to institutions and wealthy investors. It is just in the last few decades that it has been available to the ordinary investor through mutual funds. With an investment as small as $250, you can hire a mutual fund manager who earns $300,000 a year.

2. Diversification. A mutual fund can reduce business risk by creating a portfolio of many different securities. This is called diversification. Remember the Rule of Five (see page 44). The average investor would have a difficult time accumulating a portfolio of securities as diversified as that of a mutual fund. A mutual fund allows you to diversify with relative ease and low cost.

3. Liquidity. There are primarily two different types of funds available: *Open-end* funds—traded directly by the mutual fund investment company, and *closed-end* funds—traded on an exchange, just as a stock is traded.

An *open-end* mutual fund can be bought and sold at any time from the investment company. You receive the current value of your portion of the fund. This value is known as the net asset value (NAV) and is computed at the end of each business day. You can find the NAV published each day in the financial sections of most major newspapers. It is the total value of all securities owned by the fund at the day's market close, divided by the number of shares outstanding (those held by investors).

For example, let's say that a hypothetical fund owns just three different securities:

> 1,000 shares Big Biotech
> 1,000 shares Computer Wizards
> 1,000 shares Corner Grocery

At the end of the day today, shares of Big Biotech closed at $25, Computer Wizards closed at $44.50, and Corner Grocery's last trade was $33. Total value of the fund is:

Big Biotech:	1,000 shares x $25.00	= $25,000
Computer Wizards:	1,000 shares x $44.50	= $44,500
Corner Grocery:	1,000 shares x $33.00	= $33,000
Total:		**$102,500**

If the fund has issued 5,000 shares to investors, each share has an NAV of $20.50 ($102,500 ÷ 5,000 = $20.50).

Now watch the NAV change as the value of the underlying securities changes. Tomorrow the closing prices of the securities your fund owns are as follows:

Big Biotech:	1,000 shares x $26.00	= $26,000
Computer Wizards:	1,000 shares x $42.00	= $42,000
Corner Grocery:	1,000 shares x $33.50	= $33,500
Total:		**$101,500**

Now, each share of the fund has an NAV of $20.30 ($101,500 ÷ 5,000 = $20.30).

A mutual fund is always ready to redeem shares. A request to liquidate generally locks in that day's closing NAV. You will be issued a check five business days later.

Moneywise Tip

There is never any guarantee that the NAV will be equal to or greater than the price you paid on your initial investment.

Closed-end funds issue shares only once (rather than every time an investor purchases) and those shares trade on a stock exchange. Their NAV is determined in the same way as *open-end* funds, but their *share price* is determined by supply and demand and may be greater or less than their NAV, just as the price of common stock may be different from its book value. Buyers of *closed-end* funds often choose those that trade at a discount to NAV, hoping that the price will rise to the NAV in the future.

4. Variety of investment objectives. There are many funds available for every possible investment objective and you have more choices than ever before. On the next page is a sample of the different investment objectives that can be fulfilled in any level of your Personal Pyramid.

5. Flexibility to change your objectives. Mutual fund companies often manage a group of different funds, called the fund *family*. The *family* generally contains funds with different objectives such as bond funds, stock funds, balanced funds, money market funds and possibly international funds. Each has its own managers, but shares the same administrative and marketing staffs. While your main interest in choosing a particular fund is that fund's success in meeting its objectives, a good fund family is an important secondary consideration.

The advantages? As your needs and objectives change you can sell one fund and buy another without the hassle of receiving and sending checks, and without paying new commissions, if the commission rate on your first fund was

THE MUTUAL FUND INVESTMENT PYRAMID

PRECIOUS METALS
SPECULATIVE STOCK

SPECULATIVE

INDUSTRY-SPECIFIC
AGGRESSIVE GROWTH
INTERNATIONAL

AGGRESSIVE

BLUE CHIP
GROWTH & INCOME
CORPORATE BOND

MODERATE

CAPITAL PRESERVATION
INSURED MUNICIPAL BOND
U.S. GOVERNMENT SECURITIES

CONSERVATIVE

MONEY MARKET

MOST CONSERVATIVE

equal to or greater than that on the second fund. This can generally be done with a phone call. There may be a small administrative fee.

In addition, you can invest the dividends and/or capital gains from one fund into another. For example, if you are living on the dividends provided by a mutual fund, have the dividends invested directly in the money market fund of the fund family if it allows check writing. Then you can earn interest on it immediately—no mailing time!

Moneywise Tip

Transferring from one fund to another within a family is considered a taxable event.

---

6. Accessibility. Mutual fund shares are easy to buy. You can buy most mutual funds from a broker and you can buy many directly from the mutual fund company. Brokers who are compensated by commissions will prefer to sell *load* or commission-charging funds and may resist recommending a *no-load* or a non-commission fund.

No-load funds are generally purchased directly from the fund through the mail or by telephone. You must perform your own analysis on a no-load fund. Use the nine remaining questions in this chapter to analyze a mutual fund purchase or to evaluate the recommendation given to you by a financial advisor.

It is also easy to create a periodic investment plan with most mutual funds. Many will automatically withdraw an investment amount from your checking account every month. Others will allow you to send in small amounts on your own schedule. Why do this? First, because it's good to get into the habit of saving and investing every month. When you get your paycheck, pay yourself first. Second, by investing the same dollar amount every month you will accomplish something called *dollar cost averaging*.

Dollar cost averaging is a plan that eliminates the difficult decision of *when* to buy by investing a fixed amount at regular intervals, regardless of price changes.

The advantage? You buy more shares of a security when the price is low, thus reducing your average cost. A plan helps you resist the temptation to invest large amounts when markets are roaring (possibly at their peaks) and to invest nothing during bad times (when prices are low).

The disadvantage? This plan can offer a false sense of security when an investment's price drops. You must keep an eye on the fundamentals of each individual security.

Mutual Fund Dollar Cost Averaging			
Month Bought	Amount Invested	Share Price	Shares Bought*
JAN	$200	$10	20
APR	$200	$8	25
JUL	$200	$9	22.22
OCT	$200	$11	18.18
TOTAL	$800	$38	85.40
Avg share price: $38 ÷ 4 = $9.50			
Avg share cost: $800 ÷ 85.4 = $9.37			
*Assumes fractional share purchases			

7. Regulation. All funds are regulated by the Securities and Exchange Commission (SEC) and by law you must receive a prospectus *before you buy*. The prospectus describes the fund, its charges and expenses, the securities that it may purchase, and any rules for liquidating or transferring.

All funds must provide shareholders with periodic reports of performance and holdings. Additionally, you should receive an annual statement detailing dividends and capital gains received. These must be reported annually to the IRS and are taxable to you.

---

28. Where can I find objective, third-party information about a mutual fund?

All mutual funds publish sales information and prospectuses to inform potential investors about their funds. However, this literature is designed to persuade you to invest in the fund and may emphasize the positive while leaving the negative in very fine print. An independent source, with no vested interest in your purchasing the fund, is the best place to obtain comparative information.

Independent rating companies and financial magazines analyze thousands of funds and print the resulting information in a format that allows you to compare total returns and other valuable information. They will also generally print their opinion of the fund's risk and performance.

Who publishes such analyses? One of the most popular rating services is *Morningstar Mutual Funds*. This service analyzes more than 1,200 mutual funds and updates each report approximately every five months. Its reports include historical total returns, comparisons with other mutual funds and with the *S&P 500*, current holdings, and an analysis of performance. A subscription to *Morningstar Mutual Funds* costs $395 ($55 for a three-month trial), or you can generally find it in your public library.

Standard & Poor's Corporation (S&P) and Lipper Analytical Services also publish a book of reports on approximately 765 mutual funds, known as *Mutual Fund Profiles*. This report contains performance compared to the current market and prior up-and-down markets, and 1-, 5-, and 10-year total returns. A subscription costs $132, or you can usually find *Mutual Fund Profiles* in your public library.

In addition to the rating services, several financial magazines publish mutual fund rating issues. Look for *Forbes, Business Week, Financial World, Money,* etc. We encourage you to give more credence to a fund's 10-year total return than its three-month or one-year total return.

Now that you know why you might be interested in a mutual fund and where you can find objective data, what are the questions to ask about a specific fund? Begin with Chapter 4, then ask the following questions.

29. What are the mutual fund's objectives?

There are mutual funds to meet almost *any* investment objective, appropriate for any of the five levels of your Personal Pyramid. You can find fund objectives in the prospectus or in an independent report. Because the categories are broadly defined, read the fine print. For example, a fund labeled "growth" could belong in the moderate, aggressive or speculative level of your Personal Pyramid.

What is its rating?

In other words, how does an independent source rate this mutual fund? For example, *Forbes* rates funds separately in up and down markets on a scale from A to F.

Business Week uses a system of arrows. *Morningstar* awards from one to five stars. While the ratings from these and other services should not be the only criteria considered, they do provide an effective way to narrow the field before you analyze more closely. Remember, these ratings are based on historical performance, and do not necessarily predict future performance. As *Morningstar* explains, "Our rating system is more descriptive than predictive." No matter whose ratings you follow, make sure that you consider both long and short time periods.

30. How old is the fund?

While past performance is not necessarily indicative of future performance, it is the only thing we have to go on. Choose a fund that has been in existence for at least five years, and preferably 10 so that you have sufficient data to analyze. Otherwise, consider it a speculative investment, regardless of its stated objective, until the fund has a five-year track record.

31. How large is the fund?

What are the total assets of the fund?
There are small, medium and large funds. Those with less than $1 billion in assets are small; more than $5 billion, are large. Anything in between is medium-sized. There are advantages and disadvantages of each. Large funds have the ability to spread expenses over a large amount of assets, thus reducing expenses as a percent of the total assets. (The principle of economies of scale.)

Theoretically, small funds have at least two advantages over large funds when choosing and trading securities.

1. Because of their enormous size, very large funds must make large investments. This sometimes prevents them from investing in the stock of small, rapidly growing companies. Often these companies have very little stock outstanding or their stock doesn't trade actively. Large funds may not buy the stock because they can't get enough. Small funds can.
2. Stock prices are determined by supply and demand. Orders are filled in the sequence in which they are received. Thus, a fund that buys a large number of shares may pay a higher average price than one that buys a smaller number.

Do the advantages of being small outweigh the disadvantages? The managers at funds like Vanguard Windsor must believe so, because they closed Windsor to new investors. The managers at Fidelity, who operate the famed Fidelity Magellan must not think so; Magellan's huge size (more than $22 billion on Jan. 28, 1993) certainly does not appear to have had a negative effect on its performance.

32. What are the historic total returns?

Total return combines current yield (or dividends) and price change. Many investors who buy funds with current yield in mind neglect to consider falling share values, which cause loss of capital and create lower total returns.

For example, a fund with an annual current yield of 7 percent and capital appreciation of 5 percent (total return of

12 percent) is preferable to a fund with a current yield of 11 percent and capital loss of 3 percent (total return of 8 percent).

Always judge mutual funds by total return, not current yield, even if your objective is income.

Which would you rather own?

Current Yield	7%	11%
Capital Gain/Loss	+5%	-3%
Total Return	12%	8%

Look at the 10-year and 5-year annualized total returns. What do these figures mean? The "annualized" total return reflects, given the *actual returns* over a 10-year period (each year's results being different) the *average annual return* (as if each year's results had been the same). It is computed mathematically from the value of the fund at the beginning of the period and the value (with dividends reinvested) at the end of the period. It is easy to have one good year. To perform well consistently is much more difficult.

Next, examine the individual yearly total returns for the same periods. You can find out how volatile the fund is from these figures.

Then, compare total return to market averages and to the total return of other mutual funds with similar objectives. For a stock mutual fund, compare total return to the total return of the *S&P 500*. For bond funds, use a bond index, such as the Lehman Brothers Government/Corporate Bond index used by *Morningstar*. Does the fund generally outperform or underperform the markets? If you find that your stock fund outperforms the *S&P 500* in good years and underperforms it in bad years, you may draw the conclusion that the fund is aggressive and volatile. (For a measure of volatility, see the discussion of beta in Chapter 8.)

If the fund does not quite reach the *S&P 500* averages in boom years, but holds its own in bear markets, you have a fund with some *defensive characteristics*, likely a growth and income fund.

Compare 5-year and 10-year total return of a fund to others with the same stated investment objective in order to identify those in that level of the pyramid with the best performance.

33. What is the price/earnings (P/E) ratio?

If the mutual fund contains common stocks, its P/E ratio is the average of the P/E ratios of all the stocks it owns. (See Chapter 8 for a complete explanation of price/earnings ratios.) How can you use this information? Compare it to the average P/E ratio of the *S&P 500* to see if your fund is more aggressive (higher P/E) or less aggressive (lower P/E) than the market as a whole. More aggressive than market averages is not necessarily bad if you are seeking an aggressive-level investment.

34. What is the turnover?

Turnover is how often the portfolio manager sells securities and replaces them with others. Turnover of 100 percent would mean that the manager sells all securities (or the same dollar value) and replaces them once during the year. The average stock fund has a turnover of 92 percent. This is important because the mutual fund manager pays transaction costs (commissions) just as the ordinary investor does for every purchase or sale. This means a fund that gains 12 percent in value and pays 2 percent in commissions has increased by a net of 10 percent for the investor. Consider what turnover of 200 percent or more does to your total return.

In addition to the transaction costs, high turnover means rapid buying and selling, *which results in the realization of capital gains.* Unless the fund is held in a tax-deferred account, such as an IRA, these capital gains are taxable to the investor in the year earned.

35. What is the expense ratio?

The expense ratio is the ratio of the fund's expenses divided by total assets. The average expense ratio for a stock mutual fund is 1.6 percent. A good guideline is less than 1 percent for stock funds; less than 0.75 percent for bond funds. You can expect expense ratios of foreign funds to be closer to 1.5 percent per year because of the costs of investing overseas. While a fraction of a percent here or there doesn't seem like much, these expenses add up over time.

Part of the expense ratio is the **management fee** that is paid to the fund managers. Many funds have a maximum and minimum percentage that can be charged. The *minimum* allows the manager to increase the fees taken as total assets invested increase; this may be considered a reward for good performance, because the fund will attract more investors when total returns are good.

The *maximum* works the opposite way. If fund managers have some bad years and many investors liquidate, total assets managed decrease. Even charging the maximum percentage, the managers could receive lower compensation if the value of the fund has declined.

36. What is the sales charge?

Legally, mutual funds may charge a commission on an investor's purchase of up to 8.5 percent. Most charge a much lower percentage and many charge no commission at all. Funds that charge a commission on the purchase of shares are known as *load* funds and those that do not are known as *no-load* funds. The battle of load versus no-load has been argued for years, with no clear winner.

Why pay a commission? If you need a broker to help you define your investment objectives and choose a fund, expect to pay for this service in the form of a commission. If you perform your own analysis and make your choice without any help, you may prefer a no-load. *The important factor to remember is how much money you keep.*

Beware of funds that appear to have no sales charge, but charge a redemption fee. This is known as a back-end load. About one in 10 so-called no-load funds carries this fee and calls it a "contingent-deferred sales charge."

Another charge, applied by 57.3 percent of all mutual funds[7], is called a 12b-1 fee. This fee is computed as a percent of total assets invested and is deducted annually from the total value of your account. For example, a 12b-1 fee of .75 percent costs the mutual fund owner 75 cents annually for every $100 invested. The 12b-1 fee may be paid to the

---

[7] Lipper Analytical Services (*Investor's Business Daily*, April 21,1992)

broker of record. This explains why a broker may urge you to hold on to a fund rather than sell—the broker makes money while you own it. Fees of 0.25 percent to 0.35 percent, annually, are reasonable. Beware of the no-load fund that charges an excessive 12b-1 of 1 percent or more. In *Morningstar Mutual Funds*, 12b-1 fees are included in the expense ratio. Because they are part of the expense ratio, total returns also reflect their deduction.

Summary

A mutual fund investor has more opportunities than ever before. There are stock, bond and money market funds available to satisfy all objectives. Generally, professional management creates opportunities for greater total returns. In addition, specialized funds allow investors to invest in certain industries like health care or energy. You can even invest in funds that have adopted certain social objectives, for example waste management or environmental companies that follow specific investment convictions.

When choosing a fund that will be a good investment for you, consider the gaps in your Personal Pyramid and how a particular fund objective might help fill those gaps. Complete your mutual fund worksheet, paying close attention to long-term total returns, expense ratios and fees. If you make all your own investment decisions, consider a no-load fund. If you need an advisor's help in identifying and choosing a good fund for you, be prepared to pay a commission up-front.

Remember, your purchase decision is not the last of it. Review your fund's total returns and compare them to returns of funds with similar objectives on a semi-annual basis.

MONEYWISE MUTUAL FUND WORKSHEET

FUND SELECTED:_____PHONE:_____

OBJECTIVE:_____RATING:_____

INCEPTION DATE:_____ASSET SIZE:_____

MANAGEMENT STABILITY:_____

RETURN	FUND	+/- S&P 500	RANK
5-YEAR			
10-YEAR			

RETURN	FUND	+/- S&P 500	RANK
YTD			
1992			
1991			
1990			
1989			
1988			

PRICE/EARNINGS RATIO (if applicable) _____

TURNOVER:_____%   EXPENSE RATIO:_____%

SALES CHARGE:_____%   12b-1:_____%

Chapter 8

Questions to Ask About Stocks

"What did the market do today?" This is usually the question most commonly asked when you think about stocks. Or, "I want to buy a stock, what is a 'hot' tip?" Sound familiar? Neither question will give you the right information when it comes to buying stock. Let's start at the beginning.

37. What is a stock?

A share of stock represents ownership in a corporation. As a stockholder, you immediately own a part, no matter how small, of every building, piece of office furniture and machinery the company owns. You are legally entitled to vote on certain decisions, such as a change in the board of directors. Generally, each share has the same voting power; the more shares you own, the greater your power.

Companies can issue two types of stocks, common and preferred. Each has its own characteristics, and trades independently in the marketplace. Owners of common stock share directly in the success or failure of the business because their dividends generally rise with profits. Preferred stockholders accept fixed dividends in return for preference in distributing dividends or payment in bankruptcy.

You buy stock to make money in one or both of two ways: through dividend payments while you own the stock, or by selling the stock for more than you paid. There is a risk that your stock price will fall below the price you paid. So why buy stocks when you can buy bonds, which have a fixed maturity value? Over the long run, the total return (dividends plus price appreciation) on common stocks has exceeded that of bonds.

38. How does my investment objective affect the type of stock I buy?

Is income my investment objective?

If so, income stocks may be for you. Income stocks have stable earnings and high dividend yield in comparison with other stocks. They generally retain only a small portion of earnings for expansion and growth, because they enjoy a relatively stable market for their products. Examples include public utility companies, international oil companies, closed-end bond funds, and REITs (real estate investment trusts.) Depending on their history of paying dividends and their S&P rating, they will usually belong in the conservative or moderate level of your Personal Pyramid.

One note of caution: While utilities are often sold as "safe" investments, many have problems with regulatory agencies that threaten their ability to continue dividend payments at existing levels. Stocks of these companies belong in the aggressive or speculative levels of the pyramid. If the dividend rate seems "too good to be true," it probably is.

Are both income and growth my investment objectives?

The stocks you have probably heard the most about for income and growth are blue chip stocks (a term introduced in 1904), named for the blue chips in poker, the most valuable. These are the older generation of stocks and the elite of industry. They are best known for their stability of earnings and their track record of paying dividends. They are bought for both dividend income and price appreciation (growth) and generally belong in the moderate level of your Personal Pyramid.

Is my investment objective growth?

If your objective is strictly price appreciation, you probably want to investigate growth stocks. These companies are generally newer companies that are growing quickly. Their revenues may increase 50 percent or more from year to year. At the same time, their earnings (profit) may be sporadic or nonexistent, due to start-up costs, research and development or rapid expansion.

Generally, these companies will not pay stockholders a dividend because they need all available cash for growth. Because of the high failure rate of new companies, the sporadic nature of their earnings, and the lack of dividends to compensate investors in the event of falling stock prices, growth stocks are considered more risky than blue chips. They may belong in the moderate, aggressive or even speculative level of your Personal Pyramid.

Consider penny stocks only if your investment objective if speculation. These are the most volatile and risky growth stocks and are considered long shots in the marketplace. Share prices are usually $5 or less. Keep in mind that if the price of a stock is only 50 cents, that is what the market (all buyers and sellers) thinks it is worth. Be very careful when considering penny stocks. They are often sold with a high-pressure sales pitch asking you to make a quick decision.

Another way to categorize stocks is by industry. Consider how that industry reacts to movements in the economy. **Cyclical stocks** are stocks whose earnings move with the economy or business cycle.

Defensive stocks, on the other hand, reflect areas of the economy not adversely affected by a recession, industries whose products or services are bought no matter what the economic condition. Defensive and cyclical stocks can be found in any level of the pyramid. However, defensive stocks are generally considered to be more conservative than cyclical stocks. (Read more about these terms in Chapter 5.)

If you are interested in owning stock, you can never learn enough. Keep reading the questions in this chapter and get all the answers you can. It would be great if we could all buy low and sell high, but unfortunately stocks are risky business and prices change every day.

39. What sources are helpful when choosing a stock?

There are several sources to use when looking for information. You can request an annual report and any current data from the company. Keep in mind that this is the company's report and is displayed in a manner to be attractive to the shareholder. A library is a good place to find *Standard & Poor's Corporate Records* and *Value Line Investment Survey*. These are very useful third-party, impartial sources. The **MONEYWISE** Stock Worksheet at the end of this chapter will organize the data you need to evaluate an appropriate stock choice.

The stock market indexes can also be useful in several ways. First, they track long-term ups and downs to help investors judge what the market is doing and when to buy and sell. Secondly, if your particular stock doesn't follow a rise in an index over time, you may question the health of that stock. For example, if you own a utility stock, it is helpful to measure its performance against the Dow Jones Utility Average (DJUA). This will at least give you a benchmark from which to start your analysis and comparisons. Following are some of the most widely used indexes:

Dow Jones Industrial Average

Interestingly enough, the average was devised in 1884 by Charles H. Dow, the founder and first editor of *The Wall Street Journal*. The Dow is based on the stock prices of 30 industrial companies and is an arithmetic average rather than a value-weighted measure. Higher priced stocks therefore can carry more weight in the Dow than lower priced ones. There are actually four Dow Jones Averages, two of which monitor specific industries.

Name	# of companies included
Dow Jones Industrial Average (DJIA) (industrial companies)	30
Dow Jones Transportation Average (DJTA) (airlines, trucking companies, railroads)	20
Dow Jones Utility Average (DJUA) (gas, electric, and power companies)	15
Dow Jones 65 (DJ65) (total of all of the above averages)	65

Standard & Poor's 500 Composite Stock Price Index

The *S&P 500* is considered to be one of the most representative measures of overall stock market performance. It originated in 1957 and is one of the U.S. Commerce Department's leading business indicators. The index follows 500 companies traded on the New York Stock Exchange (NYSE), the American Stock Exchange (AMEX) and the National Association of Securities Dealers Automated Quotations (NASDAQ). NYSE consists of the oldest and largest companies. AMEX is made up of smaller and younger companies. NASDAQ is an electronic marketplace which brokers trade with other brokers by computer or telephone, unlike what you see on the trading floors of the NYSE and AMEX. The companies listed on the NASDAQ are generally the smallest and youngest among those of the three major exchanges.

The *S&P 500* is a weighted index by market value (market price multiplied by common shares), so that each company's stock is in correspondence to its market importance. The individual investor can rely on this index for a fair picture of overall stock market performance.

40. What is the name of the company and what is its primary business?

As you investigate stocks, you will find that companies are sometimes owned by other companies. Some are held by private investors and some are public or open to any investor. Analyze a company when you have experienced its products or services. For example, if every time you go into a Taco Bell you notice that they are very busy and appear to be making money, you may want a piece of that action.

Look for information on Taco Bell. Don't be surprised if you can't find anything under that name because it, like many other companies, is owned by a larger company, PepsiCo. You could find this information in the subsidiary records of the *S&P Corporate Records* guide. Now that you know what to look for, write down PepsiCo's phone number. Call and ask for the investor relations department. Request an annual report to see the income statement, balance sheet, past performance and future plans of the company. Remember, annual reports are prepared by the company, so we urge you to compare this data with impartial sources such as the *S&P Corporate Records* or *Value Line*.

41. What are the stock symbol and recent price?

The stock symbol is the abbreviation for the company used by the exchanges. This will help you follow the stock in the newspaper or call a broker for current prices.

Compare the current price with those during the past few months and years. Also, check the *relative price strength*, which is a figure calculated by and printed in *Investor's Business Daily*. This percentile ranking (from 1 to 99) measures a stock's relative price change during the previous 12 months compared to the price change for all other stocks. A rank above 80 is good, meaning the price change was more favorable than 80 percent of all stocks.

The volume of shares bought and sold will also be indicators for when to buy and sell. It may be a good time to buy shares when the price is rising and you see an increase in daily trading volume.

Why do stock prices constantly move up and down? Supply and demand. For every buyer who thinks the stock price will rise, there is a seller who thinks it will fall. A stock price may increase for a variety of reasons, not all of which make sense.

Conventional wisdom says that stock prices rise as the value of the company increases, due to earnings growth, asset growth, etc. In reality, the whims of the market sometimes make it difficult to see a cause-and-effect relationship. The company may be profitable or have an exciting new product. Perhaps it is part of an industry that is performing well or it is the latest victim of takeover rumors in the marketplace.

Stocks may move simply because Wall Street analysts recommend them. A stock may come out one day with good earnings and actually go down in price. Why? Analysts may have predicted that earnings would rise more than they actually did. When stocks fail to reach expectations, disappointed investors often sell, which can cause the price to drop.

We have often been asked when is a good time to buy more of a stock that you already own? For many investors, it seems easier to buy additional shares when the stock price is dropping, because it is less expensive. Or is it? Why not buy more of a good thing on the way up? A good habit is to buy shares over a period of time and dollar-cost average. By doing this you go into the market at different times, buying at different prices. Remember to buy for good reasons like fundamentals and solid performance, not on emotions or hot tips.

42. What are its earnings per share (EPS)?

Earnings per share refers to the company's net income (after taxes and preferred stock dividends) divided by the number of common shares outstanding. If you are looking for growth and stability, look for a company whose EPS has steadily increased each of the past five years.

What is the rate of growth in EPS and how does that compare to other stocks you are analyzing?

What is the Investor's Business Daily EPS rank?

This rank, published in the *Investor's Business Daily*, measures a company's earnings per share growth in the last five years and the stability of that growth. The result is compared to all companies, followed and ranked on a scale of 1 to 99. A rank of 80 or higher is superior.

What have the net sales or revenues been for the last year? For the last 5 years? For the last 10 years? What is the growth rate in net sales? What are future projections?

What (if any) dividend will you receive?

Examine the current and projected dividend of a stock, especially if your investment objective is income. Study the payout over the past five years and its rate of growth. Look at the dividend yield figure. This figure is cash dividends estimated to be declared in the next 12 months, divided by the recent price.

---

43. What is the stock's price/earnings (P/E) ratio?

The price/earnings ratio indicates, on a per-share basis, how many dollars in price you will pay for each dollar in earnings. To determine the P/E ratio, divide the current stock price by its earnings per share for the last 12 months. A P/E of 15 means that the buying public is willing to pay 15 times earnings for the stock. A company's P/E is constantly changing and must be compared with its own previous P/Es and with the P/Es of other companies in its industry. Is it better to have a high or low P/E? Let's look at an example:

Chocolate Ltd. stock has a current price of $20 per share and its earnings per share (EPS) in the last 12 months was $1. Its P/E ratio is:

$$\text{Price} \div \text{EPS} = \$20 \div \$1 = 20$$

Rick's Pizza Company stock has a current price of $40 per share and its EPS for the last 12 months was also $1. Its P/E ratio is:

$$\text{Price} \div \text{EPS} = \$40 \div \$1 = 40$$

All other things being equal (which they never are), which would you rather pay for $1 per share in earnings power, $20 or $40? Of course, $20.

Moneywise Tip

In general, a lower P/E ratio is better, because it means you are paying less for earning power.

Why do high P/E ratios exist? Because of the expectation of higher earnings. Using our last example, Rick's Pizza Company, let's say buyers in the marketplace expected that the $1 in EPS would soon be $2, which would result in a P/E ratio of 20.

$$\text{Price} \div \text{EPS} = \$40 \div \$1 = 40$$

change to:

$$\text{Price} \div \text{EPS} = \$40 \div \mathbf{\$2} = 20$$

What happens if increased earnings don't materialize?

$$\text{Price} \div \text{EPS} = \mathbf{\$20} \div \$1 = 20$$

The *price* will drop in order to bring the P/E ratio into equilibrium with other stocks. That is why stocks with high P/E ratios are considered more risky. In the event that the earnings do not rise as expected, the price may drop.

On your *Value Line* report, look at the relative P/E ratio. This ratio is the stock's current P/E divided by the median P/E for all stocks under *Value Line* review. If it is greater than one, your stock has a P/E higher than average; less than one, lower than average. Because a higher-than-average P/E may mean more risk, these stocks belong in higher levels of your Personal Pyramid.

44. What is the beta?

Beta is a measurement tool for volatility. It tells how much a stock is expected to move up or down in relation to changes in the *S&P 500*. The beta of the *S&P 500* Index is fixed at 1.00, so a stock with a beta of 1.5 is expected to move up and down one and one-half times as much as the *S&P 500*. A stock with a 1.5 beta is expected to rise in price by 15 percent if the *S&P 500* rises 10 percent or fall by 15 percent if the *S&P* falls 10 percent. Stocks with higher betas belong in higher levels of the investment pyramid because of their volatility.

45. What is the return on equity (ROE)?

ROE measures how much the company earns on the stockholder's equity. Stockholder equity is book value, or, the difference between a company's assets (everything it owns) and its liabilities (everything it *owes*). To calculate a "simple" ROE, divide earnings per share (EPS) by book value per share. Higher is generally better. Compare with other companies in the same industry.

What have its total returns been? You can calculate historic total returns based on price movements and dividends. You will also want to record total return, on an annual basis, for any investments you own. To calculate total return, add the stock's price change and its dividends for 12 months and divide the result by the stock price at the beginning of the 12-month period. (See Chapter 1 for an example of total return.)

For example, suppose you buy a stock at $42 a share and receive $1 in dividends for the next 12-month period. At the end of the period, you sell the stock for $45. Total return is 9.5 percent, calculated as follows:

Dividends	$1
Price appreciation ($45-$42)	$3
Total dollar return	$4
Total return ($4 divided by $42)	9.5%*

* Does not include commission

Once you have researched a stock, your next step is to place your order. Only a broker can execute an order to buy or sell stocks. For your transaction, you can choose either a full-service firm or a discount broker (See Chapter 14). Shop around when choosing a broker and feel free to negotiate execution costs within a firm. The more you trade with a firm, the more leverage you should have in negotiating price.

Most stock trading is in round lots, multiples of 100 shares. Odd lot trades are in amounts less than 100 shares, such as buying or selling 75 shares.

There are four types of orders.

1. Market

2. Limit

3. Stop-loss

4. Stop-limit

The most common order is a **market order**. This order directs the broker to buy or sell at the best available price in the current market. For example, "buy or sell 100 shares of Jeffco at market price."

Limit orders are used when investors want to restrict the amount they will receive or pay for the investment. For example, "buy 100 shares of Mr. Fix-It at $42 or better (less)" or "sell 100 shares of Mr. Fix-It at $42 or better (more)."

If you place a buy order for Mr. Fix-It at a limit of 42 when the current price is $42.50, it will not be executed unless the market price drops to $42. If the price rises from $42.50, your order will not be executed.

Limit orders may be placed for the day or as "good until canceled." An order placed for the day will expire unless executed or canceled the same day they are placed. An order that is placed "good until canceled" will stay in effect until either executed or canceled by the investor.

There are two types of stop orders: **stop-loss** and **stop-limit**. The unusual thing about them is that they both become another type of order when the stock reaches a certain price. The stop-loss order becomes a market order and the stop-limit order becomes a limit order.

Both types of stop orders are designed to protect profits already made, and to prevent further losses if the stock price falls. They do this by setting a selling price below the current market price of the stock. A stop-loss order becomes a market order as soon as the stock falls to or through the designated price. Because it becomes a market order, not a limit order, the actual execution may differ from the "stop" price.

For example, let's say you have placed a stop-loss order at $32 on 100 shares of Bear Broadcasting. It closes Tuesday at $34.50 and after the market closes, Bear Broadcasting issues a statement that says earnings will be much lower than expected. On Wednesday, it first trades at $29. Because your order is now a market order (the price has fallen to or through your stop price) your shares will sell at $29.

If you would like to make sure that your stock is not sold below your stop price, place a stop-limit order, which becomes a limit order at the designated price. In the example given here, your stock would not sell because you have a lower limit of $32. Brokers may refuse to issue stop-limit orders for odd lots (fewer than 100 shares) and OTC securities.

It is important to become familiar with the different types of orders available. As you can see, just one word can make a difference in how or whether your order is executed.

46. What is a stock split?

A stock often splits when a company's board of directors feels that the high price of its stock is discouraging new investors. They may initiate a stock split in order to lower the price. In a split, the company gives you more shares but lowers the price of each share. For example, if the stock splits 2 for 1, the price is cut in half and stockholders are given twice as many shares. It is no different than the concept of trading a dime for two nickels. Stocks can split in any ratio such as 2 for 1, 3 for 2, etc. They can also have a reverse split such as 1 for 10, in order to increase the perceived value of a penny stock.

Summary

Use the **MONEYWISE** Stock Worksheet on the following page to analyze the value of the company and its earnings trend. As we have mentioned before, use impartial sources for your information such as the *S&P Corporate Records* and *Value Line*. You will find these very beneficial when making the final decision. If you don't know where to start, don't just trust any name, look for something new or needed in a leading industry. Go out and shop around. Talk to other people about a product or service that you have heard about or that looks interesting. This is the best "hot" tip we can offer.

MONEYWISE STOCK WORKSHEET

COMPANY_____PHONE_____

EXCHANGE_____SYMBOL_____

RECENT PRICE_____DIVIDEND_____

YIELD_____P/E RATIO_____ BETA_____

PRIMARY BUSINESS & PRODUCTS_____

EARNINGS PER SHARE		
YEAR	EPS	PERCENT CHANGE
YTD		
1992		
1991		
1990		

ANNUALIZED RATES OF CHANGE PER YEAR		
	PAST 10 YEARS	PAST 5 YEARS
REVENUES		
EARNINGS		
DIVIDENDS		

RETURN ON EQUITY (% EARNED NET WORTH)_____

Chapter 9

Questions to Ask About Bonds

47. Why buy bonds?

Andrew Mellon said, "Gentlemen prefer bonds." It is important to purchase bonds for the appropriate purpose, select them carefully, and follow through with your investment objective. Buy bonds when you want to earn a given amount of income at preset dates, and receive your principal at a predetermined maturity date. For the greatest assurance you will receive the expected income and return of principal, purchase investment grade bonds defined in Question 52. These belong in the two lower levels of your Personal Pyramid, conservative and most conservative.

Make sure you're familiar with these terms for any discussion on bonds:

The **coupon rate** is printed on the face of the bond and determines the amount of interest you are promised to receive each year. A bond with a coupon rate of 9 percent and a face value of $1,000 will pay $90 of interest per year, usually $45 in each of two payments, six months apart.

Par value is the face value of the bond, usually $1,000. The **total return** you expect from a bond will be primarily in the form of interest income. We do not recommend the purchase of bonds for quick increases in principal. These are speculative transactions.

YTM (yield to maturity) and **YTC** (yield to call) are forms of total return (See page 105, "call date"). They include both interest and changes in principal value. They can be different from the coupon rate if you pay more or less than par value per bond.

YIELD CURVE

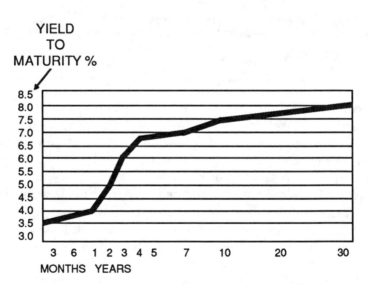

The **yield curve** is a graphic representation of current yields paid for U.S. Government securities maturing from now through the next 30 years. On the evening news you hear about the *bellwether bond,* also known as the *30-year bond* or the *long-bond.* These are all designations for the U.S. Government bond that matures in 30 years. Bonds issued by government agencies, corporations and foreign governments tend to have higher yields because they are considered to have higher risk. Yields on municipal bonds tend to be lower because of the tax-exempt status of the interest they pay. The yield curve is printed in *Investor's Business Daily,* and periodically in *The Wall Street Journal* as well as other publications.

---

48. What are the different types of bonds?

U.S. Government bonds pay interest and principal from general revenues of the federal government (including personal and corporate taxes). Treasury bills, notes and bonds are direct obligations of the U.S. Treasury.

U.S. Government Agency bonds pay interest and principal from their specific areas of operation. They are indirect obligations of the Treasury. Examples are:

- Federal Home Loan Mortgage Corporation (FHLMC, Freddie Macs)
- Federal National Mortgage Association (FNMA, Fannie Maes)
- Student Loan Marketing Association (SLMA, Sallie Maes)

Municipal bonds are issued by states, cities and other political entities (smaller than the federal government) for the purpose of financing construction, repair and special projects. Municipalities issue two types of bonds, and repayment of interest and principal is different for each:

- *General Obligation bonds* (G.O.'s), are funded by the municipality's power to impose taxes.
- *Revenue bonds* are funded by profits of specific projects such as airports, sewer districts, housing, hospitals, etc.

Which do you think pays a higher rate of interest? Revenue bonds tend to pay a higher rate because they carry higher risk than G.O.'s for the same municipality. Payment of interest and repayment of your principal are dependent upon the revenues and expenses of the project meeting their budget goals.

Corporate bonds pay interest and repay principal from the overall revenues of the corporation that issues the bond. Check the annual report of the company to learn about its profits and ability to pay you.

Convertible bonds are corporate bonds that pay interest, but have the added feature of being convertible into common stock of the company at a specific date. They may pay less interest than corporate bonds without the conversion feature, because the owner has the opportunity of principal growth between the conversion price of the stock and the market price of the stock on the day of conversion.

For example, a $1,000 bond that converts to stock at $40 per share means you will receive 25 shares at conversion ($1,000 ÷ $40 = 25). If the market value of the stock rises above 40, the market price of the bond will change with the market price of 25 shares of stock.

Zero coupon bonds have a coupon rate of zero percent. They pay all of the interest with your return of principal at maturity. Zeros are issued by the U.S. Government, municipalities and corporations. They are often used for college education, retirement planning or any time you want to designate a month during which a certain face value of money becomes available. *Buyers* like zeros because they get more face value for their investment; *issuers* like them because they can keep the interest longer and use it. Plan to buy in face value of $25,000 or more because you will usually pay too much commission if you don't. You may hear zeros referred to as STRIPs, TIGRs, CATs and other acronyms.

---

49. When will I get my money back?

Maturity date is the date when the face value will be returned to you by the issuer. It is printed on the face of the bond.

Call date is the date, before the stated maturity date, upon which the issuer can, but is not obligated to call the bond away from you, or return your principal. Why would the issuer want to do this? For the same reason you would refinance your home mortgage if interest rates fall. This is an advantage to the issuer, who will pay a slightly higher rate of interest on a callable bond than on a non-callable bond. The yield to call is the total return of the bond based on the income received before call date and the principal returned at the call date.

Moneywise Tip

Always ask if a bond has a call feature. There can be more than one call date.

You might be told, "it's callable in '99 at 101," which means, the bond could be called in 1999 and you will be paid 101 percent of face value, or, $1,010 if it is a $1,000 bond.

BOND PYRAMID

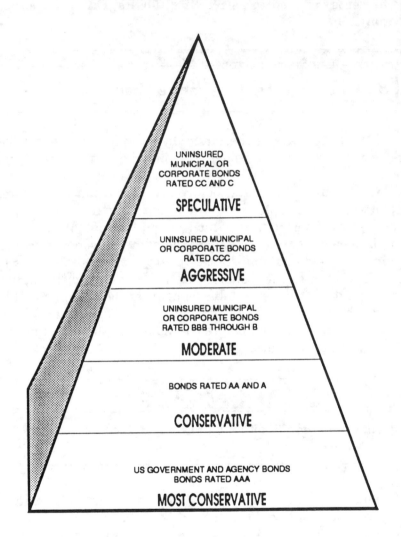

UNINSURED
MUNICIPAL OR
CORPORATE BONDS
RATED CC AND C

SPECULATIVE

UNINSURED MUNICIPAL
OR CORPORATE BONDS
RATED CCC

AGGRESSIVE

UNINSURED MUNICIPAL
OR CORPORATE BONDS
RATED BBB THROUGH B

MODERATE

BONDS RATED AA AND A

CONSERVATIVE

US GOVERNMENT AND AGENCY BONDS
BONDS RATED AAA

MOST CONSERVATIVE

50. How much does the bond pay?

The coupon rate will state the dollar amount or interest that the bond will pay. When buying a bond, ask for the coupon rate, yield to maturity (YTM), and yield to call (YTC), if callable. YTM is the total return you will receive on your investment if you hold it to maturity. YTC is the total return you will receive if your principal is refunded on the call date.

Yield Example

When the coupon rate is 9 percent, the face value is $1,000 and you pay $1,000 for the bond, your YTM is 9 percent.

If you pay more than $1,000 for the same bond, is the yield greater or less than 9 percent? It is less, because you will receive the same $90 income per year, but you have more than $1,000 invested.

If you pay less than $1,000 for the same bond, is the yield greater or less than 9 percent? It is greater, because you will receive $90 per year with less money invested.

When will you receive the earnings? Most bonds pay interest in two equal amounts, every six months. Ask when payments begin.

Zero coupon bonds and U.S. savings bonds pay all the interest at maturity.

If the bond is registered (you hold the bond certificate) payment can be made to you by check from the issuer. If the bond is "book entry form," (held by the brokerage house, no certificates are issued to you) the interest will be wired to the brokerage house and credited to your account. You can direct the brokerage firm to send you a check or to keep the money in an interest-bearing account for you.

Be aware that you can move book entry bonds at any time. You can move the registration to another brokerage firm or trust company just as you would with a stock or mutual fund or IRA account.

51. How much will the bond cost?

There are several elements that make up the total cost of a bond. When you buy a bond, you will pay principal, accrued interest and the broker's commission.

Accrued interest is the interest earned by the owner between the last coupon date and the date the bond is sold. Let's say you own a bond that pays interest on July 1 and January 1 and you sell it with a settlement date of July 28. The buyer will get the next interest check January 1, which includes 27 days of interest that belongs to you. For this reason, accrued interest is added to the buyer's purchase price. When you sell a bond, expect to receive the accrued interest; when you buy a bond, expect to pay it. Let's look at an example.

```
                    Settlement date
                    July 28
\                      \                                        \
———————————————————————————————————————————————————————————————
Interest Date                                      Interest Date
July 1                                             January 1
```

Accrued Interest		
	Buyer Pays	Seller Receives
Purchase price	$1,000.00	$1,000.00
Commission to broker	$10.00	
Accrued interest (9% X 27 ÷ 360 Days)	$6.75	$6.75
Total price	$1,016.75	$1,006.75

The above example illustrates a corporate bond which bases accrued interest on a 360 day year.

Bonds are generally marked up just like merchandise in a department store. The brokerage firm purchases the bond, adds a commission and quotes you the total price.

You can expect to pay between $5 and $20 in commission per $1,000 par value of most bonds you purchase. If you ask for a specific bond issue that is difficult to find, or if you buy less than $5,000 par value, expect to pay between $20 and $30 per $1,000 face value (or more, if the firm has a minimum commission).

In the following table the "true" example is one where the brokerage firm has purchased the bond, marked-up the price, and sold it to the new owner. The commission it makes is the difference between its purchase price and yours—the sale price. Sometimes people tell us "I don't pay a commission on the bonds I buy." This is false because it is not likely the brokerage firm makes the transaction and does not get paid. As you can see in the "false" column of the table, just because you pay face value does not mean the brokerage firm did. If that were true, they would be working for free.

What You Pay for a Bond

	True	False
Coupon	9%	9%
Par Value	$1,000	$1,000
Price paid by brokerage firm	$990	$1,000
Commission	$10	None
Total	$1,000	$1,000

It is fair to ask what commission you are paying and to have it stated on your confirmation.

Moneywise Tip

It is neither legal nor ethical for a seller to both mark up a bond and charge a commission.

Also, ask if the seller has an inventory of these bonds, or if he or she had to shop the market to find them. If they have an inventory, they need to get rid of them, so ask to pay a lower commission.

A word of caution about buying bonds. As you can see, it is not difficult to select a quality bond with a maturity date and yield that is suitable for you. The commissions you pay for long-term bonds are modest, 0.5 to 2 percent.

For this reason, we recommend you do not buy mutual funds specializing in long-term government or municipal bonds for three reasons:

1. A benefit of mutual funds is to diversify away business risk. For U.S. Government bond funds there is little business risk (risk the business will fail and not return your principal). You are guaranteed the return of the par value of a U.S. Government bond at maturity. Insured municipal bonds have little business risk. If the municipality fails to pay interest and principal, the insurance company, for example MBIA, is expected to cover it.

2. You can pick good bonds and hold them in your own account after paying a commission between 0.5 percent to 2 percent. Why pay a mutual fund a sales charge between 3 and 5 percent to do the same thing?

3. The purpose of owning bonds is to receive income. Therefore, there is no reason to pay a management fee of 0.5 percent or more every year on a portfolio of bonds when you buy them for income and hold them to maturity. There is nothing for the fund to manage other than receiving the checks every six months and mailing one-sixth of it to you each month. Buy individual bonds and *save another 0.5 percent or more every year.*

An exception is a situation in which you want monthly income or have a small amount of principal to invest. If you want monthly income, expect to pay for the benefit with the fees mutual funds charge. There is nothing wrong with that, just be aware of what you are paying for and why.

A less expensive alternative is unit investment trusts that buy bonds and hold them to maturity. Sales

111

commissions and management fees are low because bonds are not traded in the portfolio.

---

52. What is the risk? How is the bond rated?

Are my principal and interest guaranteed?
Timely payment of interest and principal is guaranteed by the U.S. government on its bonds.

The payment of interest and principal on municipal bonds depends upon the municipality. The strength of a municipality might be evaluated by Moody's or Standard & Poor's.

The top four categories for each rating service are considered "investment grade," hence, suitable for those with a primary concern for preservation of principal—widows, retirees, orphans, fiduciaries, etc.

Timely payment of interest and principal is promised by insurance companies that insure municipal bonds. Ask if the bonds are insured and check the rating of the insurance company that insures them. Go to the reference rooms of the public library and check the following five sources for insurance company ratings:

A.M. Best Co.
Duff & Phelps, Inc.
Moody's Investors' Service
Standard & Poor's Corp.
Weiss Research, Inc.

For example, if the rating is A++, A+ or A by A.M. Best you can be reasonably sure the insurance company is strong. A.M. Best has a 900-number (900-420-0400) if you want to save yourself a trip to the library. There is a charge for 900 number calls.

Bond Rating Services		
Moody's	**S & P**	**Meaning**
Aaa	AAA	Bonds of the best quality, offering the smallest degree of investment risk.
Aa	AA	Bonds of high quality with slightly higher long-term risk.
A	A	Bonds with a strong capacity to repay interest and principal. Margins of protection may be slightly lower than in Aa or AA.
Baa	BBB	Bonds of medium-grade quality. Security currently appears adequate.
Ba	BB	Bonds with a speculative element. Moderate security of payments; not well safeguarded.
B	B	Bonds with greater vulnerability of default. Little long-term assurance of payments.
Caa	CCC	Bonds of poor standing. Issuers may be in default (not making interest payments) or in danger of default.
Ca	CC	Bonds with high risk; often in or near default.
C	C	Moody's lowest bond rating.
-	D	Bonds that are in default. (S & P only)

Moneywise Tip

Check the ratings from at least three services. They perform their appraisals at different times and each has unique criteria they use to spot trouble.

Is there business risk (risk the business will fail)?

Corporate bonds and uninsured municipal revenue bonds carry the greatest business risk. With corporate bonds, the promise to pay interest and principal is as good as the credit of the corporation. With uninsured municipals, the promise to pay is only as good as the municipality's ability to collect tax revenue (G.O.) or to successfully run a project (revenue bond). Uninsured municipal bonds carry the risk that the municipality's funds are mismanaged and taxes cannot be generated to repay you; or, that the facility did not meet its revenue and expense budgets.

Corporate bonds are not guaranteed. They are like a promissory note to you from the company that issues them and are as good as the company. The return of your principal investment in a corporate bond is dependent upon the solvency of the company at the maturity date of the bond. For this reason, it is important to review the annual report of the company each year and follow your investment.

Corporate bonds are not insured by insurance companies. Never accept the statement "they are guaranteed (or insured) by the company that issues them." This statement is misleading at best, and fraudulent at worst. Corporate bonds are for those who can tolerate a little more risk and who want a little higher return. If you are tempted by the risk of high promised returns with junk bonds, just remember—while it's true that "If you don't bet you can't win, ...you can't bet if you lose all your chips."[8]

---

[8] Larry Hite, Founder, Mint Investment Management Company.

Is there inflation risk (decline of purchasing power)?
This is a risk of all bonds and of any investment that returns a fixed dollar amount at maturity. Remember, you buy bonds for income and safety of principal. There are other investments, such as common stock or real estate, that protect you from inflation risk. This is why it is a good idea to own both fixed-income (bonds) and growth (common stock and real estate) investments.

Is there liquidity risk (loss of total return with rapid conversion to cash)?
With investment grade and insured bonds, there is little liquidity risk. Junk bonds (high coupon rate) tend to be less liquid. U.S. Government bonds can be sold in an instant through your broker, 24 hours a day, anywhere in the world. Municipal bonds are slightly less liquid, but in most cases, can be sold on any given day. Corporate bonds can be highly liquid (from strong companies in large blocks) or quite a bit less liquid (from weak companies in small blocks.)

Is there interest rate risk (risk of reinvestment at lower rates to stay in the same level of the pyramid)?
All bonds carry interest rate risk. You do not know when you purchase a bond whether you will be able to invest that money at a higher or lower rate when the bond matures. You do not know whether market interest rates will rise, causing the value of your bond to fall.

Moneywise Tip

When interest rates rise, bond prices fall, but this is not a reason to sell. As long as the interest is being paid and the safety rating has not changed (putting your principal at risk), hold your bonds to maturity as planned.

Callable bonds have greater interest rate risk than noncallable bonds because the issuer is more likely to call the bonds away from you when interest rates are lower on the call date. Then you reinvest at a lower rate.

53. Will I pay taxes on the interest?

You can expect to receive income in the form of interest payments from bonds. Interest is generally taxable in the year you receive it, with a few exceptions that will follow. You could have a taxable capital gain at maturity if you paid less than face value for the bonds. The capital gains from all bonds are taxable by the federal, state and local governments that impose taxes. For this reason, we believe it is improper to say a bond is "tax-free." While your income may be tax-exempt, a capital gain is taxed by all.

Zero coupon bonds generally do not generate a capital gain when you receive both the interest and principal at maturity. However, be aware that for taxable zero coupon bonds, even though you do not receive the interest in cash, the interest you earn is credited to you and reported to the IRS annually. You must pay taxes on it each year. Interest you earn but do not receive during the year it is earned is said to "accrete."

Convertible bonds pay interest until converted to stock, after which time the stock may pay dividends.

Is the interest federally, state or locally tax-exempt?
The income of U.S. Government and agency bonds is exempt from state and local taxes. *It is one reason those in high tax brackets buy government bills, notes and bonds rather than CDs, which are fully taxed.* Note the difference in the "money you keep" below.

One Year Investment

	CD	U.S. Govt. Note
Coupon rate	4.10%	3.90%
Interest on $1,000	$41	$39
Less federal taxes at 28%	-11.48	-10.92
Less state taxes at 6%	-2.46	--
The money you keep	$27.06	$28.08

The CD's advantage in coupon rate of 0.2% became an after-tax *disadvantage* of 0.102% or $1.02.

The income from municipal bonds issued in the state where you live is exempt from federal and state taxes, hence the term, double tax exempt. The income from municipal bonds issued in the city were you live is exempt from federal, state and local taxes, and is said to be triple tax exempt. (See Question 8, Chapter 4 for another example of the money you keep versus the money you make with municipal bonds.)

In general, bonds themselves arc not tax-deferred. Exceptions are Series EE U.S. Savings Bonds. If you hold the bond in a tax-deferred account, such as an IRA, the income and capital gains are tax-deferred until you withdraw the funds from the account.

There is also an alternative minimum tax (AMT) that applies to some forms of tax-exempt income. Ask if income from your investment is subject to AMT and ask for a written explanation of the ramifications. Then, check with your tax advisor before buying. Remember, it is the money you *keep* that counts!

54. Where does this bond fit on my Personal Pyramid?

Many people consider bonds to be "safe." That is not necessarily true. Bonds can belong in any of the five levels of the pyramid. Investment grade bonds are those with one of the top four ratings by Standard & Poor's or Moody's (See Question 52). AAA and Aaa-rated bonds are in the most conservative or conservative levels. AA, Aa, and A-rated bonds are conservative. Those bonds rated BBB, Baa, BB, Ba or B are moderate. Junk bonds are those rated Caa or CCC. They belong in the aggressive or speculative levels. You are at significant risk for repayment of your interest or principal. Remember the principal of total return.

U.S. Government Treasury bills, notes and bonds, and Ginnie Maes and U.S. Government agency bonds such as Fannie Maes and Freddie Macs are most conservative.

Municipal bonds insured by a top-quality company are in the conservative level. Uninsured municipal bonds might be in the conservative, moderate, aggressive or speculative levels. It depends on how or if they are rated by an independent service. Corporate bonds can be in the conservative, moderate, aggressive or speculative levels. They are as good as the credit rating of the corporation issuing them.

55. Do I have a balanced portfolio with the proper percentage of my investible funds in each level of the pyramid?

Check to see if you own too much of one issue. You don't want your entire corporate bond holdings to be in the same company, nor all your municipal bonds to be from the same municipality, or for the same purpose.

Generally, you buy bonds for the conservative and most conservative levels of your Personal Pyramid. You may buy higher yielding bonds for their high interest rates, as long as you are aware of your potential loss of principal from business risk.

56. When should I sell bonds?

If the rating of the issuer by S&P, Moody's, A.M. Best, etc., changes, watch the business of the issuer carefully and consider if you need to sell. Otherwise, follow your original plan to hold them to maturity.

Often people are asked to buy bonds "because interest rates are going to drop and the bonds will increase in value." Who do you think makes the most money if you buy and sell bonds quickly; you or the broker?

Moneywise Tip

Do not buy bonds strictly for price appreciation or, in other words, just to turn a quick profit.

Summary

Select bonds because they fill a gap between your Goal Pyramid and your Personal Pyramid and because their quality rating and maturity date are appropriate for you. Invest your bond dollars carefully. The **MONEYWISE** Bond Worksheet on the following page will help.

MONEYWISE BOND WORKSHEET

ISSUER_____

TYPE_____ RECENT PRICE_____
(Municipal, Corporate, U.S. Govt. etc.)

USE OF FUNDS/PURPOSE OF ISSUE _____

DATE ISSUED_____ COUPON RATE_____

CALL DATE(S)_____ MATURITY DATE_____

YIELD TO CALL_____ YIELD TO MATURITY_____

DATES CHECKS ARE ISSUED_____

PYRAMID LEVEL_____
(Most conservative, conservative, moderate, aggressive, speculative)

BOND RATING_____ BY_____

INSURED BY_____ THEIR RATING_____

TAX EXEMPT:
FEDERAL_____STATE_____LOCAL_____

TAX BRACKET_____ AFTER TAX YIELD_____

SUBJECT TO ALTERNATIVE MINIMUM TAX_____

NOTES_____

_____

Chapter 10

Questions to Ask About Annuities

Are you looking for a short-term place to park your cash? Are you an investor who needs to keep your money liquid? If so, then investing in annuities is *not for you*. However, if you are a disciplined saver who seeks tax relief, or an investor looking for retirement income, keep reading.

Who should invest in an annuity? The investor who is concerned with deferring taxes and having adequate funds for later in life. Consider an annuity only after you have made the maximum contribution to any IRA, 401(k) or SEP plan available. Otherwise, you will pay too much in fees for the privilege of tax deferral. As with all investments, you need to become fully educated about annuities.

57. What is an annuity?

An annuity is simply a contract between you and an insurance company that offers tax deferral. You pay a sum of money or make periodic payments and in return receive regular payments for life or for a fixed period of time. You don't pay taxes on income or capital gains earned by the annuity until you withdraw your money or begin to receive payments.

58. Who sells annuities?

Annuities are sold by brokers, bankers and financial planners as well as insurance agents. Anyone selling an annuity must be insurance-licensed in your state.

59. How am I taxed on an annuity?

An annuity is a tax-deferred investment. You do not pay taxes on investment earnings until you start receiving the income. In theory, your money grows on a tax-deferred basis during your high income tax-bracket years. You could be in a lower income tax bracket when you receive the income, thus, pay less in taxes.

As with an IRA, you cannot withdraw money from an annuity before the age of 59½ without incurring a penalty. After the age of 59½ you can postpone paying taxes by *annuitizing;* that is, converting your assets into a stream of monthly income. Then, only the portion representing growth or interest income is taxed at your current tax rate, as you receive it.

60. What is the difference between an annuity and life insurance?

Annuities and life insurance are not the same. An annuity provides a steady stream of income to you *while you are alive*. A life insurance policy *pays upon your death* to your named beneficiary.

61. What are the basic types of annuities?

There are two basic types of annuities: fixed and variable. With a fixed annuity you are paid a fixed rate of return that is guaranteed for a specific time period, usually one year. After the guarantee period is over, the insurance company tells you what the new rate will be. The new rate can change, depending on the general direction of current interest rates and the company's earnings on your money. You should receive a notice stating the new time period and new rate each time the rate paid to you will change. Most fixed annuities have a *floor* or guarantee below which your return will not drop. This floor is often tied to the current U.S. Treasury bill rate.

Moneywise Tip

Make sure that if you renew, you receive the same rate offered to new customers.

Variable annuities work like mutual funds within tax-deferred accounts. Your premiums are invested in mutual funds managed by the insurance company. Select one of the company's mutual funds based upon your investment objective. Your return varies depending on the portfolio performance, hence the name variable annuity.

A variable annuity has more expected total return, along with more risk, than a fixed annuity. Remember, the higher the return you want to achieve, the more risk you must be willing to take. Variable annuities are riskier than fixed because your principal is not guaranteed. With a variable annuity your returns can fluctuate causing possible loss of principal.

With a variable annuity your premiums can be invested in stocks, bonds, real estate, money market instruments, mutual funds, etc.

With either a fixed or variable annuity, you can select either a *single* premium (you make a one-time payment), or an *installment* or *flexible* premium (you pay in stages over time).

An *immediate* annuity, in which payments begin almost at once, is often used by those who receive a lump sum payment from a company pension plan. With a *deferred* annuity, no payments are made until at least a year or more after you have paid your premium.

62. When and how do I get my money back?

You won't get your money until you reach age 59½ unless you are willing to give up 10 percent to the IRS in penalty fees. Your money can be returned to you in several ways: a lump sum, regular monthly payments, or as lifetime income with a stream of monthly payments. Payments will vary depending on the amount you have contributed, your age, the length of time your money has been compounding, and the rate of return you have received. When the time comes to receive your payments (annuitize), you have five choices:

Fixed-period annuity means you will receive monthly payouts for a set number of years.

Fixed-amount annuity sets monthly payments until the principal is exhausted.

Life annuity means monthly income will be paid until you die.

Joint life and last survivor annuities are designed to provide monthly income until the second spouse dies.

Life annuity period certain means lifetime income is guaranteed for a minimum number of years (10 to 20). If you die before the period has elapsed, your beneficiary will continue to receive payments for the remainder of the period.

Keep in mind that taxes must be paid on all interest and gains in excess of the amounts you paid in. The objective of annuities is to let the money compound tax-deferred when you are in a high tax bracket, and to get it back when you are in a lower tax bracket.

Cashing in your annuity before age 59½ *can* be expensive. In addition to the penalty of 10 percent imposed by the IRS for early withdrawal, many insurance companies impose a surrender charge when you take out more than 10 percent of your assets in one year during the first several years of the contract. These charges vary from company to company and can be substantial, typically 6 percent but as high as 15 percent if you withdraw during the first year.

Thereafter, the fee may be on a sliding scale declining to zero percent or no penalty. Here is an example of how a typical policy surrender fee could work:

Annuity Redemption Fees						
Before end of year	1	2	3	4	5	6	7
Surrender charge	6%	5%	4%	3%	2%	1%	0%

The above example shows that if you surrendered your policy in the first year, the penalty would be 6 percent, 5 percent in year two, 4 percent in year three, etc. In other words, it would take seven years before you could get your original money back without a surrender penalty. This is known as a "declining sales charge." The combination of surrender charges and a 10-percent IRS penalty for early withdrawal makes an annuity a long-term investment.

Moneywise Tip

You can make a tax-free exchange into another annuity. This is called a 1035 exchange and is similar to an IRA transfer.

Sometimes, putting money into an annuity can be a much simpler process than getting money out. Find out the fees required for redemption before you buy. Be aware of all sales charges and surrender charges before you invest your money.

Also, look for a plan that has a "bailout" clause so that you can cash out with no surrender charge *if* the insurer lowers the renewal rate by more than 1 or 2 percentage points below the initial rate. This feature may cost you a lower initial interest rate; say, 6.5 percent without the clause compared to a 6-percent contract with a bailout advantage. The sacrifice of one-half point could be worth it.

63. How do I select the right company?

Annuities are not federally insured, protected or guaranteed. They are only as good as the insurance company representing them. Your benefits depend on the company's financial strength, which you can check with an independent rating company. One such company is A.M. Best. The highest rating it gives is an A++. *This rating is on the insurance company itself, not the annuity.* A.M. Best's insurance reports can be found at libraries and in some insurance agents' offices.

Additional protection is provided in those states that have guaranty funds. If one insurer goes bankrupt, the state assesses charges against other insurance companies in the state to cover investor losses. Call your state insurance commission to determine if you live in one of these states. (Most states have such protection). Coverage is generally limited to $100,000 per life insurance policy or annuity. Find out before you have to—before it is too late!

The tax-deferred advantages of an annuity do not come cheaply. Sales charges, surrender fees, management costs and other expenses can greatly reduce your total return.

One publication that compares different insurers' ratings, interest rates and charges is called the *Annuity*

99 Great Answers to Investment Questions

Shopper, a 50-plus page report updated four times a year. Each issue updates the financial ratings of more than 150 different fixed and variable annuity policies. It reports each policy's current interest rates and performance, issue ages, penalties and surrender charges. One issue costs $24; a quarterly subscription of four issues is $45. It is designed to help sell annuities through U.S. Annuities Brokerage. Write to: U.S. Annuities, 81 Hoffman Road, Englishtown, NJ 07726 (800-872-6684).

You can also find variable annuities with superior historical performance by reading the performance data compiled by Lipper Analytical Services or Morningstar in *Morningstar Variable Annuities Sourcebook*. An agent selling you a policy should have and be willing to share with you the latest ratings and surveys. Don't ever be afraid to ask the insurance company what its current A.M. Best rating is. It is also a good idea to check the rating periodically, since insurance companies can be downgraded. Companies that have filed for bankruptcy, may at one time have had an A.M. Best A++ rating! Also, if the issuer is a subsidiary of a company, get the rating on the subsidiary because it could be different than that of the parent company.

64. How does the seller make money?

Sellers receive up to an 8-percent "load" or sales charge for annuities, 4 to 5 percent is a fair commission rate. Sales literature may say, "No commission! All your money goes to work for you." Ask the salesperson how much *compensation* he or she will receive (commission, general agent fees, bonuses) on your transaction. Ask who pays it. It comes from somewhere, probably from the difference between what the insurance company makes on your money and what they pay you.

For example, if you purchase a $50,000 annuity with a 5-percent sales charge (commission), that equals $2,500 to the agency selling the product. Sales charges of all kinds should be fully disclosed to you. Many times they are not unless you ask for a complete explanation. See Question 74 for more on how insurance salespeople are compensated.

Summary

Be sure to read the contract very carefully. It is often a good idea to have your accountant or independent financial advisor review it as well, and make certain you understand the answers to these questions:

- What is the current rate of return?
- What were the rates paid for the last five years?
- How long is the rate guaranteed?
- How is the rate determined?
- What are the bond ratings in the portfolio? (Select a policy with bonds rated A, AA, AAA from Standard & Poor's for the highest safety.)
- What other investments are in the portfolio?
- How long has the insurance company been selling this particular annuity? What is its rating from A.M. Best, Moody's or S&P?
- Does your state have a guaranty fund? If so, what is the limit?
- Does your state insurance department have any information on the insurance company?

These questions will help you make sure no stone is unturned when it comes to your money and investing. It is up to you to get the answers, because they will change periodically. The questions won't.

ANNUITY PYRAMID

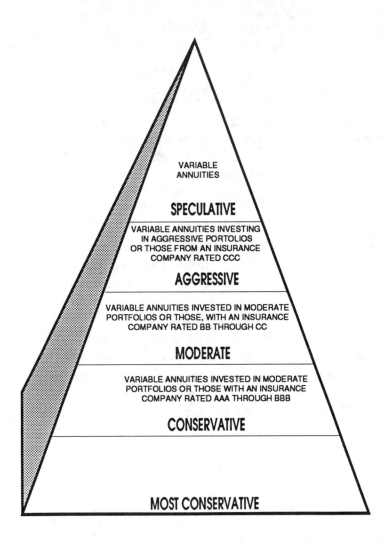

VARIABLE
ANNUITIES

SPECULATIVE

VARIABLE ANNUITIES INVESTING
IN AGGRESSIVE PORTOLIOS
OR THOSE FROM AN INSURANCE
COMPANY RATED CCC

AGGRESSIVE

VARIABLE ANNUITIES INVESTED IN MODERATE
PORTFOLIOS OR THOSE, WITH AN INSURANCE
COMPANY RATED BB THROUGH CC

MODERATE

VARIABLE ANNUITIES INVESTED IN MODERATE
PORTFOLIOS OR THOSE WITH AN INSURANCE
COMPANY RATED AAA THROUGH BBB

CONSERVATIVE

MOST CONSERVATIVE

Chapter 11

Questions to Ask About Options

Options are very complex investments. As such, they should be traded only by the sophisticated investor. If you are new to the concept, this chapter will provide an overview of the way options work. It may require several readings; don't get discouraged if you don't understand immediately. If you do consider buying and selling options after reading this, do so only with an experienced investment professional you trust.

Moneywise Tip

When it comes to investing, remember that bulls make money, bears make money, but hogs get slaughtered.

Options offer the investor an opportunity to leverage small amounts of capital into much larger sums. An option contract is simply the *right* to buy or sell, within a certain time frame, 100 shares of stock. Not all stocks have options, but many of the most actively traded stocks and the major stock indexes do.

The risk involved in options is that option buyers and sellers can easily lose the entire amount of their original investment, and sellers (also referred to as writers) can lose *even more*.

Options are a short-term strategy, since the longest time period for exchange-traded options is nine months. Except in cases where the investor uses options as a hedge, they are purely speculative and are used as a *trading, not an investing* instrument.

You can see why options belong in the speculative level of the investment pyramid.

65. What are *puts* and *calls*?

A **call** option gives its owner the right to buy (call away) 100 shares of stock for a given price within a set period of time. For example, an IBM April 50 call gives its owner the right (not the obligation) to buy 100 shares of IBM for $50 per share through the month of April (we'll get to the specific date later).

A **put** option gives its owner the right to sell (or put to the buyer) 100 shares of stock for a given price, within a set period of time. An IBM April 55 put gives its owner the right (not the obligation) to sell 100 shares of IBM for $55 per share through the month of April.

In this example, IBM is the underlying security, April signifies the expiration date, and $55 is the strike price. You can find out more about each of those from the following questions.

66. What is the underlying security?

The underlying security is the stock subject to being purchased or sold. In the two previous examples, it is IBM. The act of using the call to purchase shares or the put to sell shares is called "exercising the option."

67. What is the strike price of an option?

The strike price is the specific price per share at which the option owner may buy (call) or sell (put) the underlying security.

For an IBM June 50 call, the strike price is $50 per share. Strike prices are set at five-point intervals for stocks trading below 100, and at 10-point intervals for stocks trading over 100.

68. What is an expiration date?

This is the last day on which the option may be exercised. Options expiration dates are standardized.

All options expiring in a given month expire on the Saturday following the third Friday of the month. Exchange trading halts at the close of the trading day the Friday before.

69. What is the premium?

The premium is the price you pay for an option. The premium initially goes to the writer of the option to compensate him or her for potentially having to give up control of the stock. In a liquid options market the premium may go to a person who previously purchased the option and chooses to sell, rather than exercise it.

The amount of premium is the sum of two factors:

1. *The intrinsic value (if any) of the option*
2. *The time value of the option*

The **intrinsic value** is the money you would make if you exercised the option at the current price. For calls, it is the market price of the underlying security less the strike price of the call. For puts, it is the strike price of the put less the market price of the underlying stock.

For example:
You own an XYZ March 40 call—the right to buy 100 shares of XYZ at $40 per share. A share of XYZ is currently trading at $42. How much money would you make if you exercised it immediately and then sold the shares in the open market?

stock value	$42
less strike price	- $40
intrinsic value	$2 per share

You own an ABC April 55 put—the right to sell 100 shares of ABC at $55 per share. A share of ABC is currently trading at $51. How much money would you make if you purchased the ABC shares in the open market and then exercised your option?

strike price	$55
less stock value	- $51
intrinsic value	$4 per share

That is a pretty logical way to determine the value of the option. However the premium or price of the option is usually higher than this. That is due to time value. The **time value** is the portion of the premium (cost of the option) that exceeds the intrinsic value. The time remaining on the life of the option and the possibility of the stock price increasing (for a call) or decreasing (for a put) within that time period will create time value. It will logically be higher in more volatile stocks or stocks that show a definite trend in either direction. All other things being equal, time value will decrease as the option nears expiration. This is why options are known as *diminishing* investments.

In our last two examples let's find the time value. The XYZ March 40 call has a premium (price) of $3. We have already determined an intrinsic value of $2, so its time value is $1 ($3 - $2).

The ABC April 55 put has a premium of $7. With an intrinsic value of $4, its time value is $3.

To put it all together:

Call

stock value	$42
less strike price	- $40
intrinsic value	$2 per share
premium	$3
less intrinsic value	- $2
time value	$1

Put

strike price	$55
less stock value	- $51
intrinsic value	$4 per share

premium	$7
less intrinsic value	- $4
time value	$3

---

70. What does "in-the-money" mean? "Out-of-the-money?"

Options that have intrinsic value are in-the-money. Both of the options in our last two examples were in-the-money.

Out-of-the-money options are those with no intrinsic value, just time value. For example, an XYZ April 55 call is out-of-the-money when XYZ is trading at $50. An ABC June 35 put is out-of-the-money when ABC is trading at $38.

---

71. Why buy options?

If you've gotten this far, you can see that options are very complex. Why bother? Why not buy simpler types of investments? Because options allow the investor the leverage of spending a small amount of money to control a larger amount of stock. Using an example (prices do not include commissions), say that on August 15, you expected XYZ stock (price $33.25) to rise in value. You had two choices:

- Invest $3,325; buy 100 shares at $33.25 per share, or
- Invest $150; buy an XYZ November 35 call option. The premium is $1.50 per share, or $150 for the call option to purchase 100 shares.

Assume you make your choice, and afterwards the stock price advances. On October 15, XYZ is trading at 36 7/8 and the call is trading at 2¾. If you bought the stock for $3,375 you can now sell it for $3,687.50. If you bought the option for $150, you can now sell it for $275.

By buying the call, you have a higher total return on your money.

	Call Option	100 Shares
Purchase price	$150	$3,325.00
Sale price	$275	$3,687.50
Profit	$125	$362.50
Total return	83%	11%

It works the same way with puts. As you can see, you don't have to exercise the option in order to make money. In fact, most options traders do not exercise their options. They just plan to sell the option.

One danger in this method is timing. You may be very right about a stock, but wrong about the timing. If the price did not rise until *after* the November expiration date, your call would expire worthless and you would lose $150. If you had purchased the stock instead, and decided to hold it, you could profit from a price increase after the November expiration date of the option.

72. In what other instances might you buy options?

There are two popular ways of using options that are less risky than the ordinary buying and selling of puts and calls. We mention them here because while they have their benefits, they are sometimes recommended by unethical brokers in order to generate commissions. If you undertake either of these strategies, be sure that you understand both the upside and the downside as well as the costs involved.

The first strategy is to hedge or protect yourself against losses. Hedging is just like buying insurance. You buy insurance on your home and belongings hoping you won't have to use it. But in case of a disaster, it is very beneficial.

For example, let's say in November you purchased 100 shares of XYZ, a very volatile stock, at $62 in November (see line 1 of example on page 141). You expect it to rise but would like to hedge against the possibility (you can't be right all the time) that it might fall. Buy an XYZ January 60 put for $4.50, which will cost $450 (line 2). Your total cost for the shares ($6,200) and the put is $6,650 (line 3). You then have the right to sell your 100 shares for at least $60 per share through the Saturday following the third Friday of January (line 4), limiting your possible loss to $650 (line 5).

- *In what cases would this hedge be a good idea?*

    If it helps you to sleep better.
    If the price of 100 shares drops more than $650 or $6.50 per share (Scenario A).

- *In what cases would this hedge not be a good idea?*

  If the stock price drops less than $6.50 per share (Scenario B).
  If the stock price rises (Scenario C).

  Actual transactions would include commission costs.

Another instance in which you can use options as a hedge is in selling *covered* calls. This strategy involves selling a call on shares that you own, which means selling someone else the right to buy (call away) your shares at a certain price within a certain time period. This is most often done when you believe that the price of your stock will not change or may drop slightly.

The *objective for the call seller* is to collect the premium from the buyer and have the option expire worthless if the stock does not rise above the strike price. While this is one method for increasing the current returns from your stocks in the form of premiums received, it also limits your potential gains. You should never sell a call unless you are perfectly willing to sell your shares for the named strike price.

Keep in mind that if you make a practice of selling covered calls, something undesirable may happen. As your good stocks rise in value, they will be called away, causing you to sell them. The stocks that do not rise in value will not be called away, and will remain in your portfolio. You end up selling the well-performing stocks and keeping the laggards—it's like pulling out the flowers and leaving the weeds.

Summary

Trading options requires discipline from you and the advisor with whom you choose to place your transactions.

Options are very volatile and their prices can change in a matter of seconds. These are speculative investments, so be aware of the risk for the "expected" reward.

As a broker, one of *MONEYWISE* partners traded options for her own account on a regular basis. One day she left for a 45-minute lunch; her Coca-Cola options doubled in value and returned to their original price while she was gone. Now you can see how quickly money can be made and lost in the options market. The moral to the story is: If you trade options, make sure your broker eats lunch at his or her desk!

PUT Options as a Hedge

	100 Shares + PUT Option	100 Shares
(1)Purchase stock	$6,200	$6,200
(2)Purchase PUT	$450	$0
(3)Total cost	$6,650	$6,200
(4)Minimum sale price	$6,000	$0
(5)Maximum loss	$650	$6,200

Scenario A: Stock drops to $52

Exercise PUT	$6,000	
Sell Stock		$5,200
Loss	$650	$1,000

Scenario B: Stock drops to $57

Exercise PUT	$6,000	
Sell Stock		$5,700
Loss	$650	$500

Scenario C: Stock rises to $75

Sell Stock	$7,500	$7,500
Gain	$850	$1,300

Selling Covered Calls

Buy 100 shares of XYZ at $50 per share and sell a December $50 CALL for $5

Purchase price	$5,000
Premium received on CALL	-$500
Break-even/ lowest sale price without loss	$4,500
Strike Price/max sale price	$5,000
Premium received	-$500
Maximum return before expiration	$5,500

<u>Scenario A</u>: **Stock price does not change; hold stock**

	Purchased Stock and Sold CALL	Purchased Stock
Premium on CALL	+$500	-0-
No sale, no exercise	-0-	-0-
Gain	$500	-0-

Selling Covered Calls

<u>Scenario B</u>: Stock drops to $40; Sell

	Purchased Stock and Sold CALL	Purchased Stock
Purchased stock	($5,000)	($5,000)
Premium on CALL	+$500	-0-
Sale at $40	+$4,000	+$4,000
Loss	($500)	($1,000)

<u>Scenario C</u>: Stock rises to $60; Sell

	Purchased Stock and Sold CALL	Purchased Stock
Purchased stock	($5,000)	($5,000)
Premium on CALL	+$500	-0-
Sale at $60		+$6,000
Stock called away at $50	+$5,000	
Gain	$500	$1,000

143

Chapter 12

Questions to Ask About Life Insurance

Insurance protects you against losses you can't afford. You pay a price (premium) to the insurance company, which agrees to cover losses you incur—whether it's homeowner's insurance covering fires and burglaries, car insurance covering auto accidents or life insurance covering death. Insurance is different from investments, which provide you with income and purchasing power.

Moneywise Tip

Keep your insurance budget separate from your savings and investment budget. Those who use insurance as an investment or a savings vehicle can pay too much for it and receive too low a total return on their money.

Think of it this way: You probably wouldn't plan to use an investment to cover the costs incurred from a car accident and a resulting lawsuit.

On the other hand, you should not expect your insurance to act like an investment, making you money with a competitive total return. Insurance policies are your peace of mind when you get in your car or leave your house. Otherwise, one extraordinary medical need, one fire, one liability, and your investments or savings could quickly be exhausted.

What is confusing is all of the different types of coverage and policies available for your needs. No insurance policy covers every possible risk, so it's important to examine insurance products carefully and learn the questions to ask before buying.

73. What types of insurance coverage do I need?

Think first about what you want the proceeds to do. Then consider how much money that will require. Only then are you ready to talk with a salesperson about "how to get there." It makes a big difference in how much, and what type of policy you purchase.

The table on the next page lists different types of insurance and the purposes they serve:

Moneywise Tip

Avoid confusing sentiment with need.

99 Great Answers to Investment Questions

Type of Insurance	Purpose
Life	Replace income in the event of death
Health, major medical, medicare supplement	Provide capital for health care expenses
Disability	Replace income in the event of disability
Long-term care	Provide income to pay for long-term care
Auto and theft	Provide capital for replacement of property
Liability	Provide capital in the event of negligence
Homeowner's	Provide capital for the replacement of property
Credit Life	Provide for payment of consumer debt in the event of death
Mortgage	Provide payment of mortgage in the event of death
Umbrella	Provide for occurrences not normally covered by other policies

Here are some questions to ask:

If the proceeds are to replace income, have I explained that to the beneficiary and discussed how the proceeds should be invested to provide that income?

If the proceeds are to pay a mortgage, is the amount appropriate for my current mortgage balance?

If the proceeds are to provide a gift to charity, would the charity be better off if I contribute the same amount to them each year rather than premiums?

Or, if I invest the premiums in a moderate-level mutual fund and leave the account to the charity in my will, do they stand to receive more than if I put the money in the hands of the insurance company?

Life insurance may be purchased to provide an income for dependent survivors, to pay off a mortgage, to pay off debts, or simply to provide cash for burial expenses. If you purchase life insurance to provide an income for your family upon your death, there may be no need for the same amount of life insurance after retirement. If you purchase life insurance to pay your mortgage in case of your death, you will not need it after you have paid for your home. You can see why it is important to review your insurance needs every year to determine how they have changed, what you no longer need, and what you might need to add.

Like any other item you purchase, the price-to-value relationship of life insurance is important. It is more difficult to obtain comparative information about life insurance because reference books like *Morningstar Mutual Funds* and *Value Line* (stocks) from impartial sources are not available. Let's compare term or "temporary" insurance and whole life or "permanent" insurance.

Term life insurance protects the owner for a specified amount of time (term). Upon renewal of each term, the insured must meet specific health requirements. It will pay the death benefit only when the insured dies during the term of the policy.

This is the cheapest type of life insurance, offering the greatest amount of protection per premium dollar. As there is no cash value build-up, the entire premium goes toward the specified death benefit. While ordinary term life policies are considered temporary, a convertible policy can be converted into a permanent policy with the same company.

Cash value policies such as whole life, universal life, variable life, modified life, limited payment life, etc., protect the owner for the "whole life" of the insured. Whole life policies are designed to build cash value for the policy owner in addition to paying a death benefit.

A cash value policy is essentially a term life policy and an investment account packaged together. As with most types of packaging, there are extra costs involved. We generally recommend that you purchase term life insurance to meet your death benefit needs and invest additional funds elsewhere.

If you are contemplating using a variable cash value policy to invest because the funds in the investment account grow tax-deferred, ask yourself the following questions:

1. *Have I contributed the maximum that I can to IRAs and 401(k) plans, both of which offer tax-deferral of earnings, generally with much lower fees?*

2. *Have I compared the historic (not projected) total returns of the policy's investment account with those of a good mutual fund?*

   (Paying taxes on excellent performance may be better than tax-deferral on mediocre or poor performance.)

You will not need all types of insurance. For example, credit life and mortgage insurance are forms of life insurance. If you want coverage to pay these balances, a less expensive choice is to purchase one life insurance policy with a death benefit equal to the total of your consumer credit and mortgage balance. The advantage is that you pay less for the total coverage with one policy than with several, and the proceeds are paid to your chosen beneficiaries rather than to your creditors.

74. How much life insurance do I need?

Use this simple formula if you are purchasing insurance to provide income for your dependents in the event of your death. Most people need to generate approximately 80 percent of their income for surviving dependents. There are dozens of complicated formulas requiring thought and planning, but this one is suitable for most people.

For example: If you earn $50,000 per year, you need to provide $40,000 for your survivors ($50,000 x .80).

Assuming that the principal will earn an average of 5 percent over time, what sum of money will provide an income of $40,000? The obvious question that comes to mind is, "For how many years?" Because you don't know when you will die or for how long your dependents will need the income, assume that it will be needed indefinitely. In other words, we must find out what sum of money can produce $40,000 annually, without being consumed in the process.

$40,000 income to be replaced = $800,000 principal
x 5 percent (to solve for the $800,000, divide $40,000 by .05)

You need $800,000 of insurance to replace your income if the principal is to remain intact. If you are willing to have your beneficiaries use both principal and interest, eventually exhausting the settlement amount, have a financial advisor calculate the amount of insurance you need. It will, of course, be lower.

---

75. What does insurance cost? Where should I buy it?

The cost of insurance depends upon what you are insuring, the risk category for which you qualify, and the commissions and distribution costs paid by the company to its brokers and agents and employees.

Always ask how much the seller is *earning* when you buy a policy, and what is the source of payment. This will help you determine whether it *meets your needs to buy* or *meets the agent's need to sell*. Note the difference between asking how much commission you pay and asking how much they will earn. There are many undisclosed fees, all of which you pay for with your premiums. You are entitled to know what they are. The price you pay includes the commission but there are other earnings for the seller: general agent fees, incentives, etc.

Term life insurance offers the lowest premium for the greatest amount of coverage. Commission can be up to 50 percent of the first year's premium and a small percentage each year thereafter.

Cash value life insurance has higher premiums than term because you are paying not only for the death benefit, but you're also paying into an investment account.

Ask what the cash value will be at the end of the first year. If it is zero, or close to zero, your entire first year's premium is being used for commission and expenses. We recommend you do not purchase any policy that has a cash value after one year that is less than 50 percent of your first year's premiums.

There are low-commission companies that sell insurance over the phone and through the mail. For a comparison, we examined a $500,000 cash value policy for a 45-year old male nonsmoker, with a low-commission company and regular commission company. The premiums were about $8,700 for the first year from each company. The cash value from the low-commission company was $8,630 after one year; the regular commission company, $179. The difference is commission and distribution costs of $8,451!

How can the low-commission company afford the difference? It doesn't pay high commission to agents. It is common to pay 50 to 100 percent of the first year's premium to the seller.

Always get two or three quotes from different companies. Brokers usually work with several companies. Agents might be limited to one.

Check for low-commission insurance companies in the *Individual Investor's Guide to Low-Load Insurance Products*.

When you buy life, medical or disability insurance through your employer, don't always assume you're getting the best rate. You are buying in a group, receiving the average rate. If you are a low risk (young and healthy), you might be able to buy the same insurance at a lower cost from another source. On the other hand, if you are a high risk, you might be getting a bargain.

When buying a policy, don't rely on the "illustrations" of promised returns provided to you by sellers of insurance. They can put any attractive rate into the formula, but you have no guarantee that their earnings will be sufficient to pay that rate.

Moneywise Tip

Ask your employer about Flexible Payment Plans or Cafeteria Plans that allow you to purchase insurance with pretax dollars rather than with after-tax dollars. You can save 15 percent or more, depending upon your federal and state tax bracket.

Instead, ask for the A.M. Best 20-year dividend history report on the companies. Compare historic performance to what they are suggesting your account will earn. If there's a difference of more than two full percentage points between their historic performance and their projections, be cautious about their predictions. There is no guarantee, but historic performance speaks louder than promises.

76. Who doesn't need life insurance?

Not everyone needs life insurance. You do not need it unless you:

1. Produce an income upon which others are dependent.
2. Have debts (such as a mortgage) that would be a burden to those left behind.

Children are the most overinsured group in this country. Because they do not produce an income that others depend on, the only life insurance they might need is enough term to cover burial costs.

Once you reach retirement, reconsider your life insurance needs. If you are living on savings and investments, which will be available to your spouse should you die, there is no need for life insurance.

Many families find that as they move from the *getting growing* stage of life to the *getting comfortable* stage, they can significantly reduce their life insurance. As the children leave the nest, they no longer depend on parents' income and as a mortgage is paid, that financial burden is no longer a consideration.

---

77. What proceeds will I receive from this policy? Are they guaranteed?

Term life insurance death benefits are paid when the conditions of the policy are met on the claim and when the insurance company is solvent. This pays no other earnings.

Cash value life insurance death benefits are paid when the conditions of the policy are met on the claim and when the insurance company is solvent. The company promises to accumulate earnings for the owner in a special account. The promised earnings are not guaranteed; some policies guarantee a minimum each year, such as 2 to 3 percent.

Additionally, the owner is promised access to these earnings for the purpose of paying insurance premiums, or for a loan. In effect, the owner borrows from himself and pays interest.

Note: Ask yourself if you want to pay the insurance company an administrative fee to handle your money, especially if you expect to borrow from yourself later. Do you think you can end up with the same amount of money (or more) in your name if you buy term insurance and invest the difference in premiums in a savings account or mutual fund?

Moneywise Tip

Develop the discipline to pay yourself (into a special invest-ment account) rather than count on the insurance company to accumulate wealth for you. Keep control of as much of your money as you can.

78. How can I evaluate the solvency of my insurance company?

You should be able to get this information from the agent selling the insurance product, or check your local library. Check at least three of the following sources for rat-ings on any company you consider before you buy. It is im-portant to check the ratings at least once per year:

> **A.M. Best Co.**
> **Moody's Investors' Service**
> **Standard & Poor's Corp.**
> **Duff & Phelps, Inc.**
> **Weiss Research, Inc.**

And then check the following:

- The insurance commission of the state where you live.
- The National Insurance Consumer Healthline (800-942-4242)

Acceptable ratings are any of the top three of each, such as A++, A+, A by A.M. Best. Lower ratings are an indica-tion the company might not be able to pay your benefits when you claim them.

79. How can I evaluate my present coverage?

Things change. Once a year, decide if you have the right amount of insurance. If you have increased financial responsibilities, consider increasing your disability or life insurance coverage. If you are retired, consider lowering the amount of life insurance you carry. Consider insuring your home and belongings for *replacement value*.

80. What is the risk with insurance?

Your greatest risk is that the insurance company will not be able to pay your benefits when you claim them. This could be the result of the insurance company investing your premiums in investments that fail.

In a variable cash value policy, you run the risk that the investments in the fund do not perform as expected. Cash value insurance and annuities have liquidity risk because of IRS penalties on withdrawals before age 59½ and company-imposed surrender charges.

81. How do I file a claim and what are the tax implications?

Ask your agent to show you in the policy where this is explained. In fact, whenever you have a question about the policy, *before you buy*, ask the agent to show you the answer in the policy, to underline it and to explain it to you.

Ask your agent a few questions such as:

- *What losses are covered?*
- *How much, if any, is the deductible?*
- *How soon can I expect payment?*
- *Do I have a time limit in which I must file the claim?*
- *Does your company have a set time limit in which they must resolve my case after I have filed?*
- *If an estimate is involved, how many do you require?*
- *Under what circumstances can the insurance company cancel this policy?*

  (You don't want any surprises with your money or coverage. Read carefully and understand fully why or how a company can cancel your policy.)

- *After I do file, what, if any, is the tax implication?*

  (A death benefit is not taxable to the beneficiary. It can be taxed if it is paid into the estate of the deceased rather than to an individual or a life insurance trust. In a cash value policy, the earnings are taxed as they are paid out to the owner. Ask if you will receive your premium portion—which has already been taxed—first, or if payments to you will be 50-percent tax-paid and 50-percent taxable.)

To make your life easier, be sure to keep copies of anything you send to the company. It is equally important to keep a written file of any phone conversations, including dates and times. Over the course of filing and receiving your claim, you may speak with several individuals. You may need to refer to these notes in the future. Keep a calendar with times and dates for follow-up calls.

81. Are there any special features of the policy?

Is there an accelerated death benefit? (Also called "living benefits.")

This allows the death benefit to be used to pay the expenses of a terminal or catastrophic illness. The IRS has not yet ruled on the tax status of these transactions. Contact the IRS for a ruling in your case.

Is the company a member of the American Council on Life Insurance?

There are about 100 companies that maintain records in the case of lost policies. There is no charge to search for a lost policy, but it takes about three months to receive an answer. You can write to:

American Council on Life Insurance
1001 Pennsylvania Avenue, NW
Washington, D.C. 20004

Is a term policy renewable and convertible, without medical restrictions, to any cash value policy now offered by the company?

At the end of a term insurance period, you might want to renew at the new rate or you might want to convert to a cash value (permanent) policy if your health has changed. You should not need to pass a physical if you stay with the same company.

Summary

There are a great many groups looking out for you, the consumer. Most major insurance companies have experts on staff to help with individual questions. State-run insurance departments are required to examine the books of the insurance companies on a regular basis. There is also a National Association of Insurance Commissioners that meets several times a year and works closely to prepare unified regulations used by individual states.

Most states also have guaranty funds to protect you in the event of a company insolvency. The guaranty fund is similar in concept to the FDIC insurance fund, which covers bank insolvency. The money for the funds comes from the insurance companies performing business within that state. Even though you hope your company can pay their claims, find out if your state has a guaranty fund.

It is vital to know precisely *what* you want to insure. Everyone has different needs and wants. Take time to write down your goals, along with how much you will need and how long you need the coverage. Insurance is a buyer's market—an agent is there to serve you. You should focus on getting the best coverage, cost and care. And you should know what you are buying. The *MONEYWISE* Insurance Worksheet on the following page should help.

MONEYWISE INSURANCE WORKSHEET

TYPE OF COVERAGE_____ AMOUNT _____

TERM LIFE: RENEWABLE_____CONVERTIBLE_____

WHOLE LIFE_____UNIVERSAL LIFE_____

HOMEOWNERS_____UMBRELLA_____

DISABILITY_____ LONG-TERM CARE_____

WHAT IS THE PURPOSE OF THIS COVERAGE? _____

HOW IS EACH INSURANCE COMPANY I AM CONSIDERING RATED BY THREE OF THE FIVE RATING COMPANIES? (A.M. Best, Standard & Poor's, Moody's, Duff & Phelps, Weiss)

COMPANY_____ RATINGS_____

COMPANY_____ RATINGS_____

COMPANY_____ RATINGS_____

WHAT IS THE COST? 1)_____ 2)_____3)_____

WHAT ARE THE BENEFITS AND HOW DO THEY COMPARE?

_____

_____

WHO IS THE BENEFICIARY AND WHAT DO I WANT THEM TO DO WITH THE PROCEEDS? _____

WHAT ARE THE RISKS? _____

Chapter 13

Questions to Ask About Long-Term Care Insurance

Most people are familiar with the type of insurance that pays regular doctor and hospital bills, but now there is insurance designed specifically to pay for the costs of nursing home and at-home care. Just as you are selective when you purchase any insurance policy, you should also be particular when buying long-term care insurance. Let's take a closer look.

83. What is long-term care?

When people hear the words "long-term care," they generally think of nursing homes, but long-term care can cover assistance for chronic illness or disability. That care can be given in the home or in the nursing home. It can be for a young or middle-aged person recovering from an accident. However, most of the assistance given through long-term care coverage is used by the elderly.

84. How much does long-term care cost?

Nursing home care can be very costly: from $1,500 per month to as much as $4,000 or more, depending on the care received and the location of the home. The average annual cost of care in a nursing home facility is $30,000.[9] Depending on the insured's age and amount of coverage purchased, annual premiums on a guaranteed renewable policy range from about $300 to well over $1,000. Annual costs are expected to rise to $46,000 by the year 2000, and $135,000 by 2020. These figures are based on 5.5 percent annual growth, according to Brookings Institute in Washington.

About half of all nursing home costs are paid by individuals and their families. For many, just a few months in a nursing home could exhaust all their savings. Medicare, which is commonly thought to cover the costs of care, in fact covers less than 3 percent of nursing home costs nationwide. In order to be covered, the patient must have been in the hospital for at least three days, must enter the facility within 30 days of his or her discharge from the hospital, and the facility must meet all Medicare requirements for approval. Medicare also covers some at-home care, but only for short-term, unstable conditions.

The other half of all nursing home costs is paid by Medicaid. Medicaid is the government program for patients without money. Eligibility depends on need, and need is defined differently by individual states. Some states require

---

[9] *U.S. News and World Report*, May 1990.

that the patient be impoverished and also place a limit on the assets the spouse can retain. Generally, the states pay $30 to $100 per day for two to six years.

85. When should I consider buying long-term care insurance?

Just like life insurance, long-term care insurance becomes more costly with age. According to the Health Insurance Association of America, a policy offering $80 per day in nursing home benefits with a 20-day deductible period would cost a 50-year-old $483 per year. The same policy would cost a 65-year-old $1,135; a 79-year-old, $3,841. The advantages of buying when you are younger include the possibility that you may need care sooner than you think, and the ability to lock in lower premiums. The disadvantage is that you may end up paying more if you don't use it or use it very late in life.

When to buy long-term care insurance is a personal issue and can be very emotional. Do you buy at 50 or 70? Or not at all? Stop here and ask yourself, "Would I do better to buy growth investments with the amount I would spend on the premiums?" You can set aside, on your own, a separate account for long-term care. Consider whether you have the discipline to do that. The answers to the following questions will help you decide.

86. How does long-term care insurance work?

Long-term care insurance is designed to offer financial assistance for both at-home care and nursing home care.

Like disability insurance, long-term care policies provide a certain benefit per day for a maximum time period. Most have a waiting period before the policy starts to pay you. You can generally choose a waiting period from 20 to 100 days. Naturally, the longer the period, the lower your premium. (This is similar to choosing a high deductible on your auto insurance.)

Major policies are noncancelable. The insurance company cannot terminate your policy or raise your premium because of your age or health. It can, however, make changes to the premium for an entire group of people, such as "those living in Florida who are more than 60 years old."

87. What should I consider when choosing an insurance company?

Find out about the insurer. Check the financial health of the company underwriting the policy. Even if the coverage is through your employer, you should be confident that the insurance company will be around to pay the benefits. A long-term insurance policy is only as sound as the company behind it. That stability can change from year to year. If you ask, an insurance company should be willing to share with you its ratings and investment purchases.

88. What questions should I ask about a policy before buying?

Before buying, assure yourself that you are getting adequate coverage by getting the answers to the following:

- *What services are covered?*
  (Check to see if the policy covers skilled care, intermediate care, custodial care, home health care or adult day care. It is important to know how each of these works and how they work together.)
- *How much does the policy pay per day? For skilled care? Intermediate care? Custodial care? Home health care? Adult day care?*
- *How long will benefits last? In a nursing home for skilled care, intermediate care and custodial care? At home?*
- *Does the policy have a maximum lifetime benefit? If so, what is it? For nursing home care? For home health care?*
- *Does the policy have a maximum length of coverage for each period of confinement? If so, what is it? For nursing home care? For home health care?*
- *How long must I wait before pre-existing conditions are covered?*
- *How many days must I wait before benefits begin?*
- *Are Alzheimer's disease and other organic mental and nervous disorders covered?*
- *Does the policy require physician certification of need? An assessment of activities of daily living? A prior nursing home stay?*
- *Is the policy guaranteed renewable?*
- *What is the age range for enrollment?*
- *Is there a waiver-of-premium-provision?*
  (This provision waives additional premiums when you are collecting benefits.)
- *How long must I be confined before premiums are waived?*
- *Does the policy offer an inflation adjustment feature? What is the rate of increase? How often is*

it applied? For how long? Is there an additional cost?
- *What does the policy cost? Per year? Per month? With or without inflation protection?*
- *Is there a 30-day free look?* (You might change your mind.)

---

89. What do basic policies cover?

$80 or more per day in benefits for three years. The average stay in a nursing home is about three years. Although some policies offer lifetime coverage, the probability of needing care for more than five years is minimal.

100-day waiting period. Anyone who can pay for this type of insurance should be able to afford the first 100 days of care. A 100-day waiting period will save you money on premiums.

Inflation rider. This guarantees that you can increase your coverage as the cost of care rises. Note: You will have to pay higher premiums to get greater benefits. There are two types of inflation riders. One increases your benefits by a specific amount, such as 5 percent per year. Another bases increases on the consumer price index (CPI).

Care in custodial facilities, not just nursing homes. Known as adult congregate living facilities, these are more residential than nursing homes. People have their own rooms and eat meals in a group dining room. They're best for people who can't manage completely on their own, but don't require full nursing-home care.

Adult day care. This lets people stay at home and out of an institution much longer. Spouses or other caregivers can temporarily turn care over to others while they deal with their own lives.

Start paying when you need them. Most policies start paying when you are unable to perform two or three activities of daily living (ADLs) on your own. ADLs include: getting in and out of bed, eating, bathing, using the toilet and dressing. The greater the number of assisted ADLs that the policy requires before coverage is provided, the less desirable the policy.

Offered by companies that are exceptionally strong. The insurer should have a top rating from at least two of the five insurance rating services: Standard & Poor's Corp., A.M. Best Co., Moody's Investor Service, Duff & Phelps, Inc. and Weiss Research, Inc. You want a company that could withstand heavy losses without going under. If the money it has invested is gone, so is yours!

Offered by companies that have stringent underwriting rules to lessen the risk of loss. Such companies take a great deal of health information from applicants, check it thoroughly and reject those in poor health. If a company takes only the healthiest clients, its claims should ultimately be low, and it's unlikely the company will raise prices as quickly in the future. Of course, if you're not in the best health you'll be forced to go to a company with less stringent requirements.

Offered by companies with a long history of satisfied customers. Because long-term care policies are changing rapidly, you want a company that will provide improvements to people who have already purchased coverage.

For example, some companies allow people who own old long-term care policies to upgrade to new policies without a new medical evaluation. The new price is based on the insured's age at the time of the original application. Other companies require people who own old policies to reapply and pay rates based on their current age and health.

90. Does everyone need long-term care insurance?

No. Long-term care insurance is similar to other insurance in that it allows you to pay a known (premium) for the unknown (long-term care costs). Carefully consider the costs involved and weigh them against a personal plan of investing similar amounts in a separate account that might fund long-term care or other retirement needs.

Summary

Remember that insurance policies are legal contracts. Take your time when selecting the best policy for your needs. Read and compare carefully and be certain you understand all of the provisions. Know the difference between sales literature and the provisions of the actual policy. There is no substitute for the facts. Ask for the insurance company's ratings by A.M. Best Co. and others. These ratings are the result of careful analyses of the company's financial records.

It may also be helpful to have your doctor, children or an informed third party give you their thoughts and expertise. Good companies will want you to be an informed consumer and know what you are buying.

Chapter 14

Questions to Ask When Shopping for An Investment Advisor

How do you choose a good advisor? An advisor who will have your best interests at heart and offer unbiased advice? You can begin by scheduling a face-to-face meeting. It is up to you to interview prospective advisors for the job of protecting and carefully growing your hard-earned money.

Everyone asks investment advisors, "What is a hot investment right now?" That isn't the question the savvy investor should ask. *These are:*

91. What do you do best? What type of securities are you best at selecting?

Any advisor worth his or her salt will say "everything." However, financial advisors do specialize.

Some specialize in certain types of clients, like retirees or entrepreneurs. Others are most knowledgeable in particular types of investments, because today it is impossible to be an expert on everything. Areas of specialization include:

- Insurance and annuities.
- Fixed income securities, such as bonds.
- Growth securities, such as stocks and growth mutual funds.
- Speculative securities, such as options and commodities.

Moneywise Tip

If your prospective advisor is an insurance specialist, remember, insurance is for protection against loss:
- *loss of your life—life insurance.*
- *loss of your ability to earn a living—disability insurance.*
- *loss of your ability to care for yourself—long-term care insurance.*

If your prospective advisor specializes in fixed income securities (bonds) and you are interested in growth securities, this may not be the person for you. If your goal is growth, ask if moderate or aggressive growth is his or her forte.

If your goal is to speculate in options and commodities, find an expert in this field; commodities and options trading is very complicated and should be pursued under the guidance of an experienced advisor and *only when you completely understand the investment.*

Early on, it is important that you and the prospective advisor establish the same definitions for terms such as *defensive, long-term, cyclical, safe, conservative, moderate,* and *aggressive,* etc. Differences in definitions of these and other investment terms could cause unexpected confusion. For example, becoming more *defensive* can mean moving your entire portfolio into cash, or it can mean investing in defensive stocks, such as consumer products companies, which tend to outperform the market during poor economic periods. There is a big difference between these two!

Agree upon what an average acceptable total return will be for an account with your investment objectives. Make sure your goals are well-stated. Agree upon the time frame in which you would like to meet these goals and the time frame in which your advisor feels they are attainable.

Moneywise Tip

No one will watch your money like you will.

Never sign a *discretionary agreement* that would allow someone to make investment decisions without your approval. Even if you generally agree with an advisor's recommendations, insist that all transactions be authorized by you in advance. If you must be unavailable for periods of time, give a limited authority (this allows transactions but does not allow money to be withdrawn from the account) and specific written instructions to someone you trust other than the financial advisor.

92. What did you buy last for you own account? Why?

This might really tell you what your prospective advisor does best. If the answer to the last question was vague, you may be able to get a clearer idea here. Financial advisors tend to buy, with their own money, investments they like, follow closely and feel confident about choosing. Also, ask about personal goals and any family members he or she might advise. If there are retired parents, why not find out how he or she has advised them? If he or she is also investing for a child's college education, ask how those funds are invested. You can find out from these actions if your prospective advisor is conservative, a risk-taker, or a *responsible* risk-taker. Match this to your own objectives.

Be wary of anyone who claims to have insider information. What can that do for you? Put you behind bars, among other things. If he or she does have insider information and you act on it, you are both violating the law. If he or she doesn't really have insider information, then this is an attempt to deceive you. Both are disastrous for you and your money.

Be wary of someone who tells you about a recent big hit they made in the market. Unless your goals are speculative, this advisor's trading style might not fit with yours. This person may be a trader rather than an investor. *Traders* try to make fast money. Remember they may lose money just as fast. *Investors* try to make money soundly over time. Historically, the stock market favors investors.

93. What would you do with $100,000?

Even if you don't have $100,000, the answer to this question is valuable to you. The answer should not be an answer at all, but two (or more) questions.

- *What investments do I already own?*
- *What are my investment objectives?*

Or, in other words, *where are you now* and *where are you going*? Because only then, can your advisor best advise you *how to get there* with your $100,000.

Where you are is based on your Personal Pyramid. Your investment objectives are based on your Goal Pyramid for your financial stage of life. *How to get there* is related to the gaps you need to fill in the most conservative, conservative, moderate, aggressive and speculative levels (See Chapters 1 through 3).

The investment advisor's answer *should not* sound like, "Buy 2,000 shares of AT&T." AT&T may be a good investment, but how does the advisor know it is a good investment for you if he or she doesn't know what you own and what your specific goals are? An answer like that could mean the advisor's firm has AT&T stock in inventory that must be sold. It could mean that he or she tends to advise all customers as if their needs were all the same. Chances are, your needs are different from the next guy's; your investment advice should be, too.

---

93. How long have you been in this business? What is your background and experience?

Financial advisors are not required to have any experience, or even a license, to call themselves financial planners. They do have to be licensed with the NASD (National Association of Securities Dealers) to be a licensed securities broker. While you want to be sure that your advisor has adequate education and the proper licenses, don't put too much weight on an MBA, a doctorate, or a CFP (Certified Financial Planner) designation. While these designations indicate advanced education or testing, they have nothing to do with ethics or practical knowledge of sound investing.

To find out if there are any complaints registered against the advisor, call your state Securities Division. (To find the number, call the North American Securities Administration Association at 202-737-0900.) To communicate with the NASD, write to:

NASD
33 Whitehall Street, 7th Floor
New York, NY 10004

Or call 212-858-4400.

When searching for the right person, consider both large and small brokerage firms. Generally, the price you will pay for a security should be comparable regardless of the size of the firm. Large or small, all firms should have automated equipment and contacts on the national securities exchanges.

Larger firms may keep inventories of certain securities. This can help you if they bought at a good price and can pass that savings on to you. It is not good for you if their basis for recommending a security is their need to get rid of the inventory, rather than *your* need for a suitable investment.

95. Do you ever consult other professionals?

Brokers, planners and insurance agents are usually not investment analysts. They are salespeople. They tend to specialize in one or two areas and have general knowledge in many related areas. Just as your doctor would refer you to a brain surgeon if he or she suspected you had a brain tumor, your financial advisor should seek advice or refer you to your present accountants, attorneys and other professionals if you need expert advice.

If your broker advises complicated strategies, trusts or insurance designed to save on estate or other taxes, be sure to get a second opinion from your accountant or attorney. When investing in tax-exempt or tax-deferred securities, ask your accountant or a tax specialist whether these investments make sense for you before signing on the dotted line.

If your financial advisor refers you to a specific accountant or attorney, ask if he or she receives any compensation for the referral. Some advisors receive referral fees from other professionals, which means the referral is not necessarily an objective one.

96. May I speak with some of your current customers?

A good advisor should have plenty of happy customers who would be willing to talk with you. Ask to talk with someone whose situation is similar to yours or who has similar objectives. While the past certainly doesn't guarantee future returns, you should be able to get a good idea of how well the advisor has performed.

When you talk with this person, ask how well the advisor's recommendations have performed in the best and worst years. Ask how often the advisor calls. Does he or she call once a week or once a year? Only when he or she has something to sell? Or to update the client on an account's progress? Does he or she recommend frequent trading? Explain investment ideas well? Get a feel for how comfortable you would be if you were in this person's shoes. *Ask the referral if he or she would hire the advisor again.*

97. Will I be working with you or someone else?

Make sure that you won't be passed on to a junior person or an assistant in six months. This sometimes happens after the initial transactions. You want continuity and you don't want an administrative assistant calling you in six months with ideas he or she can't explain. Financial goals require long-term planning—moving from advisor to advisor can disrupt the process.

If your advisor assures you that you will be working with him or her, agree on how often you will be in touch and under what circumstances. It is your responsibility to let an advisor know whether you would like a quarterly "check-up" or a call every week. Everyone has different preferences; don't expect your advisor to read your mind.

Never let an advisor make you feel like you are not important enough. He or she is not doing you a favor; you are paying for a service. There is always someone who will make you feel like an important customer, no matter *how much or how little* money you have.

98. How do you charge for your services?

This is one of the most important questions you can ask. But, unfortunately, most investors fail to ask it in advance.

- *Are you fee-based?*
- *Are you commission-based?*
- *Do you charge both hourly fees and commissions?*

Fee-based planners charge by the hour and are paid whether or not you buy investments from them. Those who do not charge an hourly fee are commission-based, and earn a commission when you buy or sell, or own certain securities. Both styles of payment have their advantages.

Fee-based planners can charge from $50 to $200 per hour and should be able to tell you in advance how much time you will need. We recommend you have your records in order, take your Personal Pyramid, and have a written list of your questions and ideas (in order of priority) so you can save time and money. There isn't any reason to pay someone $100 per hour to organize your account statements.

If you have a limit to the amount you can pay, say so up front. Begin with, "I'd like two hours of your time." A good advisor will then do his or her best to prioritize the information in those two hours so that the most important items are covered. Consider taking your spouse or a family member with you, so he or she can learn too. Take notes; it is impossible to remember everything.

There are two types of commission-based brokers: discount and full-service. If you make all your own investment decisions, handle your own research, and just need someone to execute your transactions, choose a discount broker. You will pay lower commissions than with a full-service broker. Why? A full-service broker charges higher commissions in return for research and advice. If you don't need these services, don't pay for them. If you analyze your own mutual fund purchases, consider no-load funds. The sales commissions on load funds exist to compensate an advisor who helps you make your choice.

If you make some of your own investment decisions and do not trade frequently, but would like the input of ideas and research, a full-service, commission-based broker may be for you. If so, remember that these brokers generally get higher commissions when they sell life insurance or annuities and "house" brand products, such as mutual funds managed by their brokerage firm.

How do I know if my broker, planner or agent is churning (buying and selling frequently in order to generate commissions) my account?
First, calculate your total return and compare it to your investment objectives and market averages like the *S&P 500*. Who is making more money—you or your broker? Add all the commissions you paid during the year on all buy-and-sell transactions and compare the total to the gain in your account value.

What if I want to change brokers when all my securities are held at my broker's firm?
Confronting your former broker may be a situation you would like to avoid. No problem. Your new broker can give you a one-page form to sign that authorizes him or her to move your account and its contents to the new firm. You do not need to contact the former broker. Be aware that it may take four to six weeks for the transfer to occur. The responsibility is that of the sending firm and, naturally, they do not give these transactions top priority. Insist, however, that any money market funds remain invested for all except 24 to 48 hours. *Let both parties know what you expect.*

What happens when your broker leaves his or her current firm for another? If you really want to find your former broker, look in the phone book for a home number. The firm that your broker left usually will not tell you where he or she went, and your broker may not be able to contact you legally. (Many brokers sign noncompete contracts that prevent them from contacting customers if they leave one brokerage firm for another.)

Generally, after a broker leaves, his or her accounts are assigned to the remaining brokers. If you get a call, "Hi!

This is Austin your new broker," ask the questions in this chapter. *Your broker is your choice. Choose wisely.*

Tips on dealing with a broker

- Keep a journal of all conversations and transactions. If you work with a discount brokerage firm, write down the name of the broker who places your order each time you trade.

- Always have the broker repeat your order to verify your instructions.

- Periodically review both your total return and how much you have paid the broker (his or her total return).

- Never make a check payable to your broker for the purchase of an investment. Checks should always be made payable to the brokerage firm, mutual fund company or custodial bank.

- Always read your statements when they arrive. Mistakes are made, and the sooner they are caught, the easier they are corrected.

- Save all your statements. When you need this information at tax time it may be expensive and time-consuming to get copies from your brokerage firm.

Summary

Now you are ready to choose an advisor. Following these three steps will help you make the best selection:

Step 1. Interview at least three advisors. Be sure to ask for referrals from friends and family to narrow the selection process.

Step 2. Schedule appointments. Look for a comfortable relationship as well as professional fit. You will get your best reading on compatibility by meeting face-to-face.

Step 3. Ask the prospective advisor the eight questions identified in this chapter. Take notes and be prepared to answer the advisor's questions. *A good advisor will have a list for you as well.*

Chapter 15

Question 99: "Where do I go from here?"

Remember the very first **MONEYWISE** tip: "If you can't spend the time, don't spend the money." Get involved with your investment decisions. Read investment magazines like *Money*, *Forbes* or *Fortune* and newspapers such as *Investor's Business Daily* or *The Wall Street Journal*. Go to the library once a month to look at stocks in *Value Line Investment Survey*, or mutual funds in *Morningstar Mutual Funds*. It takes time, but it is your money! Get the answers! You owe it to yourself.

You can't afford to say, "I don't have time." Take it slowly and make a plan. Wouldn't you rather take time now to have more money later? Set aside a few hours each month to make the process manageable. Find out where your money is; determine if it is working as hard as you are. The only thing more important than making money is *keeping* it. No one will watch your money like you will.

Get the Word— A Moneywise Glossary

American Depository Receipt (ADR): Serves as a proxy for a foreign stock deposited in a foreign bank. It is issued by an American bank, and trading it is equivalent to trading the foreign stock.

Bear Market: A declining market.

Blue Chip Stock: A company that is known for the quality and wide acceptance of its products or services, and for its ability to make a profit and pay dividends.

Bond: Debt of a company, government or municipality in which the issuer promises to pay the bondholders a specific rate of interest (coupon) until a specified date (maturity). The bondholder is a creditor and not a partial owner, as is a stockholder.

Book Value Per Share: The asset value behind each share of stock. This is theoretically the value that shareholders would receive upon liquidation of the company.

Bull Market: A rising market.

Business Risk: The risk inherent in a company's operations.

Call: An option to buy a specific security at a designated price (strike price) within a certain period of time.

Capital gain or loss: Profit or loss from the sale of a capital asset.

Certificate of Deposit: A time deposit issued by banks. It generally has a set maturity date, interest rate and penalty for early withdrawal.

Common Stock: Securities that represent ownership in a corporation. They do not have a maturity date and may or may not pay a quarterly dividend.

Current Yield: The annual interest or dividend payment as a percentage of the current market price of a security. To determine the current yield, divide the dividend or interest by the current market price.

Dilution: The reduction in the percentage of ownership of each common stockholder through the issuance of additional common stock.

Dollar Cost Averaging: A system of buying a fixed dollar amount of securities at regular intervals. As a result, the investor buys more shares of the security when the dollar price is low, and fewer when the dollar price rises. Thus temporary downswings in price benefit the investor who continues periodic purchases.

Equity: The net worth of a company, which consists of capital stock, paid-in capital and retained earnings. Common equity is what belongs to the stockholders.

Ex-Dividend: A stock that is trading without its upcoming dividend. When a stock that is trading ex-dividend is sold, the seller is entitled to the dividend and the buyer is not. The ex-dividend date is the first day on which the stock trades without its dividend—four business days before the record date.

Face Value: Also called *par value*, this is the amount that a company agrees to pay the bondholders at maturity of the bond. This may or may not be the actual market value of the bond.

Government Bonds: Debt of the U.S. government such as Treasury bills, notes and bonds. Generally regarded as the highest-grade bonds in existence.

Liquidity: The ability of the market, in a specific security, to absorb a reasonable amount of buying or selling without extreme price changes.

Municipal Bonds: Bonds issued by a state, county, city or other political subdivision. Generally, interest received on a municipal bond is federally and state tax-exempt in the issuing state.

National Association of Securities Dealers (NASD): A self-regulatory organization of securities brokers and dealers.

National Association of Securities Dealers Automated Quotations (NASDAQ): A market for securities outside of the organized exchanges. NASDAQ (over-the-counter dealers) may act as agents or principals. Quotations on this market generally consist of a bid price, at which an investor can sell, and an offer price (higher than the bid price), at which an investor can buy. The spread between the two is the profit that the market-maker realizes.

Net Asset value (NAV): Used in relation to mutual funds and unit investment trusts. The NAV is the total market value of all assets, less any liabilities, divided by the number of shares outstanding.

New York Stock Exchange (NYSE): The largest organized securities market in the United States. Prices on the exchange are determined by supply and demand.

Overbought: An opinion about price levels. A security or the general market may be considered overbought if prices are too high or have just risen quickly.

Oversold: The reverse of overbought. An opinion that market or individual security prices are too low.

Par: For common stock, it is the dollar amount assigned to shares when the company is formed. It is often $1 and has no relation to the market price. For preferred stock, the par is the value upon which dividends are figured. For a bond, it is the face amount, the amount due at maturity.

Price/Earnings Ratio: The P/E ratio is computed by dividing the price of a stock by its earnings per share. The value of the ratio signifies how much in dollars an investor would pay to buy $1 in earnings. All other things being equal, a lower P/E ratio means a "cheaper" stock.

Prime Rate: The rate charged by banks in lending to their most credit-worthy customers.

Put: The option to sell a specific security at a designated price within a certain time period.

Record Date: The date on which a shareholder's ownership must be registered with a company in order to receive a declared dividend. The record date is four business days after the ex-dividend date.

Round Lot: Unit of trading or a multiple thereof. Generally 100 shares for common stocks and $1,000 par value for bonds.

Short Saie: The sale of a security that an investor does not own, with the intention of buying the security at a later date at a lower price.

SIPC (Securities Investor Protection Corporation): A regulatory organization that insures the customers of member firms against fraud or failure of that firm.

Stock Dividend: A dividend paid in securities rather than in cash.

Stock Split: An accounting function that increases the number of shares outstanding. As no new value is added, the market price generally drops proportionately.

Street Name: Securities that are held by a brokerage house or trust company in the name of the firm for a customer's account.

Total Return: The profit from an investment; dividends, interest and price appreciation.

Transfer Agent: The company that keeps a record of all registered shareholders, and sees that shares that are sold are properly canceled, and that shares that are purchased are properly issued.

Yield to Maturity: The total return of a bond, which takes into account not only the interest payments, but the price discount or premium that was paid at purchase. A bond purchased at a discount will have a **yield to maturity** that is higher than its current yield, and a bond purchased at a premium will have a **yield to maturity** that is lower than its current yield.

Index

99 Great Answers to Investment Questions